INTERNATIONAL EXPERIENCES IN MODERNIZATION OF THE SYSTEM OF STATE EXECUTIVE POWER

FURKAT JURAKULOV

© Taemeer Publications LLC
International Experiences in Modernization of the system of State Executive Power
by: Furkat Jurakulov
Edition: January '2024
Publisher:
Taemeer Publications LLC (Michigan, USA / Hyderabad, India)

ISBN 978-93-5872-161-4

© **Taemeer Publications**

Book	:	International Experiences in Modernization of the system of State Executive Power
Author	:	Furkat Jurakulov
Publisher	:	Taemeer Publications
Year	:	'2024
Pages	:	150
Title Design	:	*Taemeer Web Design*

Jurakulov, Furkat
International experiences in modernization of the system of state executive power [Text]: textbook / F. Jurakulov. - T.: "Renaissance", 2023. - 200 p.

Abstract

This textbook, international experiences in the modernization of the state executive power system in Uzbekistan and their socio-philosophical and political significance are disclosed. The content and essence of the reform of the local and self-government system, its place in society, and the processes of formation of our national spirituality are explained. Also, the formation of the national model of the modernization of the executive power system in the country and its prospects, the political and legal foundations of the development of the presidential institution in the management of the state power, and the philosophical views about the democratic features of the reform of the local state power system, developing a strong will, feelings of love for people and the Motherland are also described in the textbook.

This textbook, prepared from the subject "International experiences in the modernization of the state executive power system" 60112100 - National idea, spiritual foundations and legal education, was created on the basis of current qualification requirements, curriculum, approved model program in the field of undergraduate education.

Teacher's textbook, prepared for the subject "International experience of modernization of the system of state executive power" 60112100 - National idea, basic spiritual and legal education, basic practical qualification requirements, educational plan, approved standard program in the area of higher education.

Annotation

This textbook reveals the foreign experience of modernizing the system of state power in Uzbekistan and its socio-philosophical and political significance. The process of reforming the system of local self-government and self-government, its significance, place in society, the processes of formation of our national spirituality are explained. As well as the formation of a national model for the modernization of the executive power system in the country and its prospects, the political and legal foundations for the development of the presidential institution in public administration, the democratic features of the reform. The local system of state power, which is described in the textbook, provides students with a healthy faith, strong will, feelings of love for their people and Motherland are formed.

This textbook, prepared on the subject «International experiences in the modernization of the system of state executive power» 60112100 – National idea, spiritual foundations and legal education, was created on the basis of the current qualification requirements, curriculum, approved model program in the field of higher education.

CONTENTS

Introduction

1. The system of state executive power in developed countries, theoretical aspects of modernization experience

2. Models and concepts of modernization of the system of municipal (self-government) organizations

3. Modernization of the state executive power system: International and Uzbek experience

4. The process of modernization of the state executive power system in Anglo-Saxon countries

5. Modernization experience of State power system in Romano-Germanic countries

6. Modernization of the public service provision and management system: Chinese and Japanese model

7. The principle of division of state power in Uzbekistan and reforms to ensure mutual balance

8. Modernization of the executive power system in Uzbekistan

9. Modernization of the system of executive power in the country formation of the national model and its prospects

Conclusion

List of used litrature

INTRODUCTION

Nowadays, the reforms of modernization of the state administration system in developing countries are deepening more and more. Special attention is paid to the separation of powers, achieving mutual balance between society and state authorities, guaranteeing human rights and freedom, and ensuring mutual responsibility of the state and citizens to each other as the main principles in the formation of a legal state. In particular, mutual limitation and differentiation of the powers of central and local authorities, the election of heads of local executive authorities, and the provision of public control by public institutions and citizens over the activities of state organizations remain an urgent issue.

In the world, in the process of global integration, there is an increasing interest in researching the democratic aspects of the modernization of the state executive power system. The principles and experiences of the modernization of the state executive power system in the development of civil society are studied with great interest in political research. In these studies, the factors hindering the establishment of a legal state and the formation of a civil society are analyzed based on the scientific conclusions of the world experience in the field. In Uzbekistan, the modernization and further democratization of the state executive power system, including the gradual transfer of powers of the central government to local governments and institutions of civil society, and decentralization, and the research of these processes from the point of view of political science, remain one of the urgent tasks.

During the years of independence, the constitutional and legislative foundations for the modernization of the state executive power system were created in Uzbekistan. In the course of reforms, the tendency to eliminate some elements of centralized management preserved in the system of state executive power was consistently continued. In recent years, the analysis of appeals received by the public reception offices of the President of the

Republic of Uzbekistan showed the need for further democratization of the executive authorities. Therefore, in the "Strategy of Actions" for the development of the Republic of Uzbekistan in 2017-2021, the improvement of the state and society building system were defined as the main direction. The "Concept of Administrative Reforms in the Republic of Uzbekistan" aimed at the rapid modernization of the state executive power system was adopted. At the end of the administrative reforms, the aim was to create a new model of the system of compact and professional executive organizations.

Law of the Republic of Uzbekistan No. 369 of May 5, 2014, "On the Openness of the Activities of State Power and Management Organizations", Presidential Decree of the Republic of Uzbekistan No. PF-4947 of February 7, 2017 "Further Development of the Republic of Uzbekistan in 2017-2021 the Decree on the Strategy of Actions, the Decree of the President of the Republic of Uzbekistan dated September 8, 2017 No. PF-5185 "On Approving the Concept of Administrative Reforms in the Republic of Uzbekistan" and other regulatory legal documents related to the field serve as a theoretical resource.

1- THEME: THE SYSTEM OF STATE EXECUTIVE POWER IN DEVELOPED COUNTRIES, THEORETICAL ASPECTS OF MODERNIZATION EXPERIENCE

Plan:

1. *Advanced indicators of modernization of society.*
2. *Administrative reforms in developed countries.*
3. *The process of decentralization of state authorities.*

Currently, the experience of modernizing the state power of the developed Western and Eastern countries, developed by CIS scientists, is widely studied from a political point of view.[1] It is known from these studies that today the modernization of the state power system has become the basis of world civilization. For example, in developed countries such as Europe, North America, Japan, South Korea, and Australia, the processes of modernization of the state power system are being completed, while the countries that are going through the transition period are starting such reforms. During the period of independence in the Republic of Uzbekistan, the conditions for the modernization of the state power system - legal frameworks were created, and the reforms of implementing democratic processes in the system of state management organizations are ongoing. Since 2017, serious changes in this field have been implemented in the country. Shavkat Mirziyoyev, who was elected as the President in 2016, started promoting the democratic principles of modernizing society and state organizations.

The main goal of the reforms in this field is "The people should serve our people, not the state agencies, the state agencies should serve our people." based on the idea of modernization of the state power system.

Action strategy on the five priority directions of further development of the Republic of Uzbekistan: "Deepening democratic reforms aimed at improving the state and society and strengthening the role of parliament and political parties in the modernization of the country, reforming the public administration system, developing the organizational and legal foundations of public service, "Electronic Further deepening of reforms based on the tasks of "improving the government system, increasing the quality and efficiency

---

[1] Stepanova AA Sravnitelnyi analiz mechanizov vzaimodeistviya organov gosudarstvennoy vlasti i institutov grajdanskogo obshchestva: na primere Rossii i Velikobritanii: autoreferat dis. ... candidate political science: 23.00.02. - Saratov, 2009. - S. 25.; Gukova INRazvitye obshchestvenno-politicheskoi activity molodeji na osnove vzaimodeystviya organov gosudarstvennoy vlasti i institutov grajdanskogo obshchestva: autoreferat dis. ... candidate political science: 23.00.02. – Orel, 2016. – S. 22.; Pegasheva MA Vzaimodeystye organov gosudarstvennoy vlasti i institutov grajdanskogo obshchestva v sfere etnoconfessionalnykh otnosheniy: na primere Nizhnego Povoljya: autoreferat dis. ... candidate political science: 23.00.02 Vasilyeva TA Vzaimodeystviye gosudarstvennyx organov vlasti i negosudarstvennyx nekommercheskix organizatsii kak institutov grajdanskogo ob shestva v sovremennoy Rossii: tendentii, protivorechiya, perspektiv razvitiya: auto referat dis. ...doctor of political science: 23.00.02. - M., 2009. - S. 48.; Bakutina N.S. Vzaimodeystviye organov vlasti, biznesa i elementov grajdanskogoobщestva v protsesse politicheskogo upravleniya innovatsionnыm razvitiyem: avtoreferat dis. ...kandidata politicheskix nauk: 23.00.02. – Nijniy Novgorod, 2015. – S. 20.; Alyabyeva S.A. Sotsialno-politicheskiye aspekti vzaimodeystviya institutov grajdanskogo obshestva s organami ispolnitelnoy vlasti: avtoreferat dis. ...kandidata politicheskix nauk: 23.00.02. – Voronej, 2012. – S. 26.

of public services, implementing public control mechanisms, strengthening the role of civil society institutions and mass media" is aimed at the modernization of the state power system.

According to Talcott Parsons, a well-known US scientist, "in the 17th century, each of England, France and Holland took a leading position in the system of states through their national development. These three countries led the process of modernization in its early stages".[2] So, modernization processes started 3-3.5 centuries ago. However, despite this, the scientists of the present era have not come to a common conclusion in the interpretation of the concept of "modernization". That's why we turn our attention to encyclopedias in order to visualize this concept more reliably: it is defined as "Modernization is the process used to classify the process that has been going on for a long time in the world - towards the acquisition of a characteristic feature of less developed societies that is different from most developed societies. These are social changes and processes specific to development".[3] Of course, for a deeper understanding of this concept, it is necessary to know the concept of "underdeveloped society". Most scientists use it as "traditional society", and developed societies as "modern society" (or modernized society). In this case, the main factor is the denial of various innovations and their non-acceptance by people living in a traditional society.

That is why all innovations are created in developed countries. So, the differences between the developed and not so developed society determines whether different ideas, new views, new technologies, production of high-value goods or vice versa will occur.

Also, in traditional societies, scientists are connected to each other on the basis of blood relations by dividing them into separate groups and communities, which leads to a lack of strong and stable connections between these communities or groups. In this, it is emphasized that the decision made by one team does not affect other teams, that is, there is no communicative relationship. Unlike modern societies, participation of citizens is considered a participatory society, and they coordinate with each other based on consensus. In such a society, most people enter into dialogues and relationships with

---

[2] Parsons T. Sistema sovremennыx obщestv / Per, s angl. L.A. Sedova i A.D. Kovaleva. Pod red. M.S. Kovalevoy. – M.: Aspekt press, 1998. – S.76.
[3] Lerner D., Coleman J., Dore R. Modernization // International Encyclopedia of the Social Sciences. 1968. Vol. 10. – R.386.

each other, are in constant social competition with each other, and have the experience of satisfying their interests through non-governmental organizations. State authorities recognize their activity, freedom and rights.

Initially, the concept of modernization was expressed in concepts such as "anglicization" in India and "westernization" for the entire eastern societies. As a result of Westernization, "East Asian tigers" such as Japan, South Korea, Taiwan, Singapore, Hong Kong flourished economically. The spread of modernization was also caused by the rise of industrialization, which is one of its main factors.

Modern society can develop only in conditions of market economy. As the state's involvement in the market economy grows stronger, such a society loses its sense of modernity. The difference between a modernized society and a traditional society is immanent[4], which always ensures its economic renewal even in difficult conditions is the existence of mechanisms. Also, the modern society is different from the traditional society, and the civil culture of the population is high. As a result, democratic values can survive in such a society. More importantly, the process of assimilation of the democratic political culture, with the majority of the people abandoning the paternalistic political culture, is gaining momentum.

Members of modern society differ from traditional society in terms of physical, social and mental mobility, and citizens of such a society can quickly adapt to a changing social environment. Because these changes live in conditions of a high level of communicative relations, they have already mastered the instincts of feeling. Also, people's behavior is rationalized[5] in a modernized society, they are characterized by breaking free from the shackles of traditional imaginations and striving for innovations. According to T. Parsons, the process of modernization of society should go through three important revolutions.

They are the industrial revolution, the democratic process and the revolution in the field of education.[6] Of course, this concept was born during the study of the experience of developed countries in the world.

---

[4] Immanent [lat. immanence (imma-nentis) characteristic, originality] - the originality of some phenomenon, process or object is its origin from its own nature.
[5] Rationalization [lat. rational] - improvement of some methods or some work or activities.
[6] Parsons T. Sistema sovremennix obshestv / Per. English LA Sedova i AD Kovaleva. Pod ed. MS Kovalevoi. - Moscow: Aspect Press, 1998. – P. 102–116, 125–131

The need to modernize the system of state power, especially the executive power, arises as a result of the formation of civil society and the increase of citizens' activity.

However, China's experience has proven that it is possible to modernize the state power and its management even in a communist society without a civil society. But the Chinese leadership also used the experience of capitalist countries in this process: they applied market relations to their economy. Deng Xiaoping, the architect of China's modernization, developed and spearheaded the implementation of the new "Chinese Model" concept of development, combining the positive aspects of the socialist system with the economic potential of the capitalist system. He is himself, in his concept, he justified the fact that the socialist system can live based on the capitalist base as a structure.

He initially focused his policy of "building socialism on the basis of China's characteristics" to increase the welfare of the people. That is why there was no opposition to this policy in society. In particular, the conformity of Confucian teachings, imbued with the spirit of ensuring justice in the economy and state administration, to Deng Xiaoping's policy was of great importance in ensuring his success. Under the leadership of Deng Xiaoping, it began to bear fruit in almost 5-6 years. Development has accelerated in many areas of society.

The indicators of growth in industry, economy and finance started to grow at the level of developed countries. Of course, the modernization of public administration and service based on the requirements of the market economy was the main direction of the reforms in China. The intervention of the Chinese Communist Party in the economy was limited, the direct management of the economy by the state was abandoned, many ministries and civil servants were reduced, and the public service sectors of the state were expanded, and much of the public service was transferred to the private or non-governmental sector. The principles of evaluation of the civil servant's performance based on his last results have been established. Small business and entrepreneurship began to be fully supported by the state.

Modernization in China began to bear its fruits in a short period of time: the budget allocated to public administration decreased; the effectiveness of management has grown extremely rapidly; the economy, entrepreneurship and small business management have grown immeasurably since the barriers were removed; one of the main functions of state power management focused on the development of market economy relations; All for ownership and economic freedom in social conditions have been created; The flow of investments into China has increased.

It can be seen that regardless of the different ideological or state system, it is possible to modernize society and the management system of state power. The first lesson to be learned from China's experience is that in order to implement reforms to modernize society and the system of state power, it is necessary to first modernize the state administration system, that is, to decentralize it - to transfer the functions of management and public service to the lowest state organizations (the Chinese experience is described in detail in paragraph 2.3. given). In general, it is thought that the experience of Chinese modernization, which is distinguished by its uniqueness, should not be overlooked as a methodology for researching the management system of state power.

Modernization of the state power system mainly involves the implementation of administrative reforms, *decentralization of the system of central and local authorities, self-management* it is carried out in such areas as the transfer of some powers of the state power to the organizations and *non-governmental organizations,* updating and retraining *of the civil service personnel* . The concept of *"administrative reforms"* is used in two ways - narrow and broad. In a broad sense, it means implementing large-scale and deep structural changes in the public administration system, and in a narrow sense, it means implementing reforms that radically rebuild the public service sector. This direction of administrative reforms (the concept of "administrative" comes from the Latin "administrative" (administrate - management, leadership)) is called decentralization (decentralization) of state power and local authorities in Western countries.

Currently, the state implementing administrative reforms relies mainly on the experience of European countries, especially Great Britain, France, and Germany. Implement these reforms the internal reasons for the increase are the need for political, economic, social, information-communication, management and general changes. It is understood to reform by democratization of the administrative-state management, which has lost its position as a result of the decrease of trust of the political elite in the eyes of the citizens, when citizens' dissatisfaction with the work of the state apparatus appears for political reasons, when economic and social problems arise in the public sector. Economic reasons include the expansion of the civil service staffing, overspending and budget deficit.

It is said that the social reasons are due to the decrease in the quality of public services and the rise of bureaucracy. Reasons in the field of management refer to the situation where public sector management technologies fall below the level of management in the business sector. For reasons in the field of information and communication, reforms regarding the use of new information and communication for the effective implementation of public service can be included. General scientific reasons are understood as the changes aimed at putting an end to situations such as the fact that officials under the supervision of the state do not deeply study the scientific-theoretical foundations of the ever-improving management, look at it with disdain, and give little importance to the use of the potential of science in the implementation of reforms.

Decentralization reforms, which formed the basis of administrative reforms, first began in France in the early 80s of the 20th century. After a short period of time, such reforms began in Great Britain, Germany and Sweden. By the end of the 20th century, these processes began in all countries of Europe and North America. Within ten years, the ideas of narcissism spread to most of the countries of the world. These reforms began to bear positive results in a short period of time.

External (foreign and international) influence on the implementation of administrative reforms, especially changes made as a result of factors such as world integration and globalization. The desire for integration encourages the administrative reforms implemented by each country.[7]

Up to now, state reforms in most countries, no matter which direction they are implemented in, such as administrative, budget and state management, are focused on the implementation of the following goals, which are common to all of them:

- increase the quality of the budget service;
- increase the efficiency of state expenditures;
- to increase the quality of the activity and management system of the

---

[7] Dubrovin Yu.I. Administrativno-gosudarstvennoye reformirovaniye v stranax Evropeyskogo soyuza. Abstract dis. nor soisk. three. degree of Doctor of Polit. Nauk. - M., 2009. - P.15-16.

executive power and its organizations at all levels.

At the present time, reforms have been carried out on the basis of results-based management concepts in countries such as the USA, Great Britain, France, and Germany. Such new developments have spread to many countries. Therefore, as a common task in this field, improving the quality of budget services has become an urgent task for states to actively cooperate with the population.

States constantly monitor the opinions of the population in order to determine their preferences for public service. In particular, the municipal organizations of Great Britain constantly conduct surveys among the population about the quality of public services provided, their tax burden and level of compliance.

One of the tasks of implementing reforms in this area is to develop a system of regulations for working with citizens. In Great Britain, such a system is called "standards of dealing with citizens". It specifies the indicators of working with the population for civil servants. And in France, since 2000, citizens for every state institution, the guidelines and obligations for establishing relations with, in addition, the government made decisions on "simplifying many types of public services" and introduced new rules for collecting payments from citizens.

In European countries, special services have begun to be organized to provide high-quality state services. A special personal case-manager (case-manager) is allocated for job- seeking citizens. In addition to providing information about government services related to finding a job for its owner, it also collects information from all government services related to this field. Another direction in this field is to focus on increasing the transparency of public services provided to the population in developed countries and ensuring the speed of these serv Ensuring the implementation of these tasks is entrusted to the Departments of transport, regions and municipalities. Every year, they develop and present the most effective and high- quality codex indexes to the public on their official website. Also, since 2000, most western countries have established a rule for each ministry to develop and approve a service quality assessment plan.

As one of the main directions of administrative reforms in European countries, the formation of an open management system was given great importance. For this purpose, administrative activities and court proceedings have been improved. If we take the experience of Great Britain as an example of the reforms in this field, in the next decade, this country implemented administrative reforms to solve the following problems in the management system:

- the fact that business management, especially corporate management, lags behind all quality dimensions of public administration organizations;

- the increasing cost of implementing public administration functions in the environment of continuous improvement of management and information technologies;

- the existence of unnecessary positions in the state apparatus, the inability to ensure that the officials approach their duties enthusiastically, their lack of responsibility;
- the need to form an economical and efficient state apparatus is growing, the results obtained from existing management resourcesare not based on demand, the need to reform the system of evaluating their activity.

As a result of these reforms, the foundations of civil society in the British society were further strengthened, and mechanisms were formed to ensure the stability of the society. The well-being of the population has also increased significantly.

The main foundation of administrative reforms is decentralization (lat. decentralization) of public administration organizations. That is why the UN Human Development Program encourages decentralization of authorities in all countries. According to the program, as a result of decentralization, democracy will be strengthened in local areas, the independence of local self-government organizations will be ensured and their activity will increase. These processes ultimately become effective means of economic development.

The well-known Western scientist Robert Ebel expresses the importance of these processes as follows: "the Western world is a low-cost alternative to decentralization of social services. Developing countries implement it to increase economic efficiency and improve governance. The countries of the former union accept it as a natural step in the transition to a market economy and democracy. Latin America approaches democratization as a tool for democratization. And Africa sees it as the way to national unity"[8]

---

[8] Robert D. Ebel, Sirdan Yilmas. Measurement of the degree of scale decentralization and its influence on macroeconomic indicators. // Material of the conference Budgetary federalism and financial management at local level. - M.: RAKS, 2002. - P.14.

According to the experience of developed countries, decentralization means transferring responsibility for planning, management, and resource use from the central government and its organizations to the management below them.

Decentralization is inextricably linked with the concept of subsidiarity (Latin for reserve, assistant, helper), according to which functions or tasks are transferred to the lowest levels of social management.

There are three forms of decentralization - political, administrative and fiscal types, four - devolution, transfer of powers, deconcentration and divestment. Political decentralization means the transfer of political power to regional authorities from citizens' assemblies to local authorities. Devolution (in English devolution is the transfer of authority or responsibility) is the transfer of responsibility, power, resources and sources of income to local authorities in order to ensure their independence or autonomy. Administrative decentralization means making decisions on coordination and management of various social services, their resources and management responsibility to lower state authorities and self-government organizations.

Deconcentration refers to the transfer of some powers and responsibilities of the central government to local authorities while maintaining hierarchical subordination.

Deconcentration is the first step towards decentralization of management. Devolution is the redistribution of central authority and responsibility to local governments (not necessarily local units of central government). In this case, local government organizations are given responsibility, while their vertical subordination is preserved. Fiscal decentralization (Latin fiscalis belonging to the state; treasury, tax) is a more complete and transparent type of decentralization of power, which is directly related to budget practice. It also means transferring resources from the center to the regions.

So, based on the legal and political reforms carried out in our country, it is an urgent issue to study the experience of modernization of state power in developed Western countries from an analytical and critical point of view. The process of modernization of state power in Western countries cannot be assessed as a complete reality.

Because even in these countries, the need to develop new constructive ideas to ensure the cooperation of state authorities and civil society institutions is increasing more and more. The experience of countries such as the USA, Germany, and Sweden in this regard can serve as a certain political paradigm for other countries.

In this way, the modernization of the municipal system in Western countries was formed as a combination of signs of generality (decentralization) and specificity (based on national experience). Importantly, modernization processes created the basis for further development and growth of economic potential of all Western countries. Another important aspect of modernization reforms is that the civil society formed in the West in the second half of the 20th century became more refined and democratized. This situation created unprecedented conditions for citizens to exercise their rights and freedoms.

In general, in the analysis, the experience of modernization of the state power and management system of Western and North American countries, theoretical developments, methods, and various models related to modernization developed in these countries can serve as a methodology for researching modernization processes in countries undergoing a transition period. found the proof.

As Uzbekistan aims to establish a legal democratic state and a strong civil society, first of all, reforming the political system and further liberalizing it in order to ensure the cooperation of state executive authorities and civil society institutions is of priority.

Control questions
1.   What are the advanced indicators of modernization of society includes?
2.   What are "administrative reforms" in developed countries? consists of?

3.   What does the process of decentralization of state authorities include?

2- THEME MODELS AND CONCEPTS OF MODERNIZATION OF THE SYSTEM OF MUNICIPAL (SELF-GOVERNMENT) ORGANIZATIONS

Plan:

1. *The nature of the activity of self-governing (municipal) organizations.*
2. *System of municipal (self-government) organizations models.*
3. *Concepts of the system of municipal (self-government) organizations.*

While several centuries ago self-governing (municipal) [9] organizations functioned as a political organization performing lower local government functions of the state, by the 20th century they have gone through a long historical development path to becoming an institution of civil society. According to Western political scientists, the concept of "self-government" is related to the formation of the independence of citizen communities in relation to the state. According to the French thinker Alexis de Tocqueville, local self-government is such a political institution that it is a school for all citizens, not just politicians. The possibilities inherent in this institution are so high that it creates conditions for broad political participation of citizens.

Self-government organizations are an incomparable factor in the formation of elements of political culture. Ultimately, the activity of these organizations ensures the overall stability and flexibility of the political system. Or, as Tocqueville wrote, "a nation may form a free government without collective institutions, but it cannot have the true spirit of liberty."

German scientists associate the author of this concept with the name of Prussian minister Baron Von Stein (1757-1831). Stein wrote that local self-government is "an active form of citizen management of public affairs." In the sources of the 19th century, the concept of "self-government" began to be used in relation to state-republics, US states, Swiss cantons. In Great Britain, "self- governing organizations" mean conciliation courts, consultative courts and parliamentary institutions.

Local self-governance refers to activities of local importance, which are carried out by elected organizations representing the powers of the population in one or another administrative territorial unit, and their administrative apparatus.

---

[9] Munici pium (lat.) - a self-governing community.

Municipal administration is a relatively decentralized form of public administration. At the same time, it is an institution of the Russian society. The main characteristics of such governing organizations are their election and relative independence in managing matters of local importance based on the interests of the population in their territory.

Municipal management organizations also represent the elements of the state organization. But in most countries, they do not occupy a higher level than the state organizations, because most of the functions of managing the territories have been taken from them and these functions have been given to the agencies of the government and ministries. Municipal management is a separate link in the state mechanism, which is functionally related to the state administration apparatus.

At the same time, since it is a body representing the interests of the residents of its territory, it performs the functions of self-management as a community institution.

The theoretical foundations of municipal management were initially developed by the ideologues of the revolutions in Western Europe, and its nature and role are related to the ideas of local authorities and community self-government organizations in elections. The principle of the election of local authorities corresponds to the ideas of representative government, which were born as a form of action against feudal absolutism. The concept of independence of elected municipal organizations, their independence from the center in leading the affairs of rural communities and cities, expressed the functions of local self- government at the beginning of the new history, and these organizations began to be interpreted as a link outside the sphere of state interests, i.e., an institution of society.

During the 19th century, three models of interaction between the center and local self-government organizations were formed (English, French and Prussian). Today, the models based on these established traditions continue to be used in Anglo- Saxon, French (or Southern European model) and Germanic (or Northern Central European model) life.

The most exemplary of local self-government is the Anglo- Saxon model, in which the processes of self-government take place "within the local interests of the authorities". In the French model of self-government, power is (formally) in the hands of local government organizations that oversee self-government. In the German model, state administration and local self-government are combined as a single institution. The Anglo-Saxon model group includes countries such as Great Britain, USA, Canada, Australia, New Zealand, Ireland. The French model is more widely used in Italy, Belgium, the Netherlands, Portugal and some Latin American countries. Also, the local self-government organizations of Germany and Scandinavian countries have specific qualities that are not similar to the two models mentioned above. As a result of industrialization processes leading to drastic changes in the economy, the functions of local self-governance organizations also underwent major changes. As a result, their activities expanded and these organizations began to specialize in large areas. During this period, activists who were supporters of innovation put forward the views that self-government organizations consisting of small communities cannot effectively satisfy the interests of the population. Attempts to modernize like this have also caused protests from local officials. During this period, the communal model of self-government began to develop in the United States, in addition to France and Italy. Great Britain, on the other hand, is on the way to reducing large, identical units of local self-government. A number of other countries tried to follow their own "middle" path, adopting some features of both models.

The specific features of the improvement of the central state organizations, as well as the processes of their modernization, at each stage of its development, created conditions for the consolidation of specific models of the organization of mutual relations between the management organizations at the central, local and other local levels.

Of course, in these processes, the influence of the central government on the lower administrative system was also strong. Reforms on the modernization of local and self-governing organizations were carried out under the influence of the following conditions:

a) in the conditions of the supremacy of national laws;

b) as a result of attempts to take mass actions on the ground (for example, such as a wave of widespread protests);

v) In the conditions of mutual solidarity or equality of all political subjects, as in the USA, as well as the absence of clearly expressed participation of the center.

In the 19th century, the communal model of self-government began to develop in the United States, in addition to France and Italy.

Great Britain, on the other hand, is on the way to reducing large, identical units of local self-government. A number of other countries tried to follow their own "middle" path, adopting some features of both models.

At the same time, elements of civil society began to form during the reforms.

The well-known scientist DJ Leiser expressed the following opinion about this: "Federalism of the modern era did not appear until civil society became important for the political life of the West"[10]

There were also views that local self-government itself creates conditions for the formation of civil society. But at the same time, it was also observed that the values of local self- government differ from each other in different national countries. In particular, in the USA, there have been cases of adherence to conflicting values: on the one hand, the values of broad participation, pluralism and representative democracy have developed, and on the other hand, the importance of effective governance has been given importance.

Based on the theory of democracy founded by the fathers of the USA, the views that local authorities should express the will of the people, and the best way to achieve this is direct individual participation in local governance, had a strong influence on self-government reforms. Of course, such approaches were first of all founded by T. Jefferson and A. Tocqueville.[11]

In the early years of the formation of the USA, T. Jefferson was a supporter of the "small republics" system, according to which the self-governing regions should be so small that in these "small republics" every citizen should be able to directly participate in general meetings and be directly involved in political activities. As a classic example of such a system, A. Tocqueville cites the New England township[12] as an example: "If the power belongs to the people, then the people themselves must rule. This is the main principle of the republican government."

---

[10] Eleazer D.Dj. Sravnitelny federalism // Polis, 1995, No. 5. – P.108.

[11] American Federalist: Hamilton, Madison, Jay. - Benson, Chalidze Publicationis, 1990. - P.221.

[12] Township (eng.) - residential areas in a district, settlement, town, village.

Although the pluralism and representative democracy developing in the USA during this period were mainly derived from the concept of T.Jefferson, these new principles were actually a reflection of the existing values: in addition to the supporters of pluralism recognizing the place of political participation, this participation is not of individual-individuals, but wanted it to happen by competing groups.

Instead, the principles of pluralism formed in the United States were based on John Locke's views on the control and limitation of power. At that time, J. Madison, who was strongly influenced by this, wrote: "It is necessary to control and limit not only the power of the government, but also the power of the majority, as well as the power of opposing "factions".

Later, S. Huntington compares these two approaches and gives the following analysis: "T. Jefferson's views on the ideal of democracy are in direct and complete opposition to J. Madison's concept of expanded republicanism"[13]. For Jefferson, republicanism is attractive because of its closeness to people. And for Madison, it is also important because it is far from people. For Jefferson, small print media is the republican ideal in its purest form. For Madison, small republics consist of a bad form of "factionalism". For Jefferson, the main threat to republicanism is the tyranny of centralized autocracy. Madison's views on the distribution of powers and the need to introduce limits by means of "checks and balances" spread to the townships of the United States outside of New England in the 19th century, and it was expressed in the mutual distribution of executive (mayor) and representative (council) powers in American municipal government.

As a result of the wide spread of Madison's views in the United States, there was an increase in the flow of public immi grants, which tended to demand the representation of the interests of their ethnic groups in local authorities. In this way, units of political participation in municipal politics developed in the form of groups. The active political participation of immigrants went along with the processes of influence of elements of the political culture of the countries to which they previously belonged on the policy of the United States. This situation led to the formation of structures called "political machines" in the interpretation of American political science.

---

[13] Huntington S. Politichesky pryadok v menyayushchikhsya obshchestvax. - M.: Progress-Tradition, 2004. - P.28.

Municipal governing organizations are one of the components of the representative system based on their election and official position as representatives of the local population. Their activities in the economic and social sphere are of great importance for the population. In comparison to other branches of the state apparatus, bureaucratism is less common in municipal organizations. All these qualities made elected local government one of the values of democracy. Also, the municipal administration, on the one hand, exercises some powers of state administration in local areas, and on the other hand, as an institution of civil society, represents and protects the interests of the population.

During the period of classical capitalism in the early 19th and early 20th centuries, the development of local government is similar to the previous freedom and equality far removed from democratic slogans. Firstly, the elections in the formation of municipal organizations began to be limited by the increasing participation of the property-owning part of the population, real estate owners. Second, municipal organizations came under government control in order to subjugate local and group interests to national interests.

In the municipal policy of the government and parties, the principles of centralization gradually began to gain priority. With the expansion of the functions of local self-government organizations in education, communal economy and other fields, the intervention of the mar kaz in local affairs also increased.

By the 20th century, under the pressure of the state, local government lost the qualities of real local self-government, the activities of being free from the interference of the bureaucratic apparatus of the central government. Under fascist regimes in Germany and Italy, elected local government was abolished, among other democratic institutions. Reducing the powers of local administration, its dependence on the bureaucratic apparatus has become a general principle of the aspirations of the central government.

At the same time, the increasing demand for democratization of municipal management, actions such as subordinating the activities of municipal organizations to the interests of the population, as a counter- effect against the restriction of citizens' rights and freedoms, and the increasing role of the central bureaucratic apparatus.

The degree of centralization and decentralization of local government, the level of democracy in the structure of local institutions largely depended on the ability of citizens to force the central government to make concessions.

As a result of the defeat of fascism, due to the sharp increase in the prestige and influence of democratic forces, there have been positive changes in the situation of municipal organizations in a number of countries. In particular, the democratic principles of local self-government were strengthened in the constitutions of France, Italy, and Japan after the Second World War.

The consequences of large-scale urbanization processes in the United States have also influenced theories of local self- government. Political activity in the 60s of the 20th century led to the development of theories about the priority of the territorial structure of local units. Discussions have intensified about the qualities of various models in this field that are effective:

1) the effectiveness of innovation;

2) create more conditions for democratic decision-making;

3) be able to guarantee fair distribution;

4) the ability to ensure mutual cooperation for economic growth.

Proponents of enlarging local self-governing organizations cited as evidence the economic efficiency of larger structures, the inability of many types of services in small municipal structures to operate widely, the fact that large units can receive more powers, which in turn strengthens local influence in determining political direction. . They also put forward the opinion that the municipal structures should correspond to the regional economic units - then the implementation of regional planning will be effective. They also gave a negative argument that small municipalities can ensure the effectiveness of their work activities only under the influence of resources in other areas.

Those who disagreed with the enlargement of municipalities tried to prove that the living unit or the city has its own characteristics, and the economic success of municipal structures does not depend on their size or smallness. They argued that large municipal structures alienate citizens from power, and that large size does not guarantee good planning and distribution.

As one of the directions of reforming the local municipal management system, Western scientists have also conducted scientific research in the field of reforming power and management organizations in the regions of unitary states. As the conclusions of these studies suggested that the authority of municipal organizations should be empowered to supervise and coordinate the activities of lower organizations and local government organizations. In particular, the municipal system in the USA, despite the fact that it consists of small structures, has undergone some twists - the partial cooperative reform of municipalities for the purpose of forming intermediate management links was carried out in harmony with the processes of extensive urbanization and related changes. The working group of the commission of the US Academy of Arts and Sciences developed the following analysis: "The management structure should first of all adapt to the processes of urbanization. Urban growth at unprecedented rates is blinding states' viability. Their role should change in one of two directions: the states should remain within the framework of the main functional areas, or the states should become one of the forms of "city administration"[14]. But this proposal did not pay off even in the more ur Another direction of the principles of the enlargement of municipalities was to give powers to newly formed organizations (regions in France, metropolitan councils in the USA). In addition, a number of public service functions have been directly delegated to local authorities or their agencies without any intermediate management links. From the point of view of national governments, these reforms were seen as implementation of decentralization.

Functional and territorial decentralization in the doctrines of decentralization applied in practice in the French experience means "granting powers to autonomous institutions and organizations of the state that perform certain functions in the regions, in one or another administrative-territorial units."

Also, "territorial-vertical decentralization is based on the establishment of new administrative territorial divisions - regions."

Since the 70s of the 20th century, the concept of monetary management in the USA and Europe has changed significantly. Because in this period, the Western European countries began to deeply reform this sector.

---

[14] See: Menin N., Parison N. Reforma gosudarstvennogo upravle niya: international opit. Per. English - M.: Izdatelstvo "Ves Mir", 2003. - P. 405-411

Decentralization reforms soon began throughout Western Europe. One such change took place in Great Britain in 1974.

According to the concept of new changes, it was intended that the administration at the level of the commune/church communities will continue its activities in rural areas. As the largest units of local government, the legal status of the Metropolitan Council (Metropolitan) in England and the Regional Councils in Scotland has been reformed. They, in turn, were covered by district councils in regions of geographical latitude.

It was introduced that each county of the country or Scotland should consist of these district councils. Municipal administration service has been facilitated and simplified at all relevant levels.

New changes were clearly felt in cities, villages and regions.

In the seven major conurbations (Greater London, Greater Manchester, Merseyside, South Yorkshire, Tyne and Wear, West Midlands and West Yorkshire) the Country Council (Metropolitan) was reformed as a strategic body responsible for the natural and economic planning of the counties. District councils, as subordinate organizations after the metropolitan, were empowered to provide special services to the population (for example, education, service sector, road operation, housing construction, environmental improvement). However, even in rural areas, such broad structures operate, the responsibility for some specific services within them has been assigned to the Country Council (for example, education, service sector, road use, etc.).

Also, the following requirements were imposed on local self-government organizations:

- the ability to meet the needs of citizens; a means of meeting the needs of citizens;
- the legitimacy of his leadership in his community;
- different in society the ability to adapt to changes; freedom to be influenced by local conditions in relation to the specific needs and demands of their community.

In developed countries, the methods of forming municipal organizations have also developed. Article 3 of the "European Charter of Local Self-Government", adopted by the European Union on October 15, 1985, expresses this concept as follows: "Local self-government is the responsibility of local self-government organizations, based on the interests of the local population, based on the laws: the ability to manage most of the state affairs and to be able to do it realistically. These rights are exercised by councils or assemblies consisting of members elected in free, secret, equal, direct general elections. Councils or assemblies may have executive or reporting organizations. These rules do not exclude the use of citizens' meetings, referendums or other forms of direct participation of citizens allowed by law".[15]

By the end of the 20th century, the concept and content of self-governing organizations have changed a lot. Scholars such as G. Hollis and K. Plokker (experts of the European Union) interpret the concepts of local self-government, according to which "local government" includes all the following levels from public administration: "local government" - "an elected council and its organizations that represent and act in the interests of their constituents through executive organizations"; "local self- government" is "the coordination and management of the majority of public problems by democratic autonomous units of a lower level than the national government based on the interests of the local population".

In the 80s of the 20th century, local government reforms began to take place in a number of countries (Great Britain, France, the GFR, etc.). These reforms ended, if not completely, the old traditions in the organization of local government.

At the same time, the apparatus of municipal organizations in general strengthened their positions in management and reduced the functions of local elected governing organizations.

Funds allocated by the central government for various social services in the activities of municipal organizations have decreased, and the activities of local authorities in areas such as health care and housing have decreased. The evolution of municipal management, the municipal policy of the state has found its expression in the theories of local management that are widespread in modern political science.[16]

There are various theories that express the subordination of municipalities to state administration, which represent a return from the ideas of local self-

---

[15] See: Hollis G., Plokker K. Na puti k demokratcheskoy decentralizatsii: perestroika regionalix i mestnih organov vlasti v novoy Evrope. – Brussels: TACIS services DGIA European Commission, 1995. – P.13–25.

[16] See: Barabashev GV Local self-government. - M.: 1996. - S.16-21.

government. The concept of municipal management dualism [17] is characteristic for this direction.

Proponents of this theory associate the central administration's wider penetration into local life with the fact that a number of local works (for example, education, road construction) are gaining national importance. According to this theory, the municipality should perform certain management functions and leave the scope of local interests, as well as it should act as an instrument of state administration. At the same time, municipalities retain their independence in purely local affairs.

The theory of dualism of municipal administration reveals the social causes that arose as a result of the central government's attempt to deprive municipalities of their rights and independence. Thus, it is interpreted that the reason for the center's intervention in municipal affairs is to ensure the same high standards in the management of areas of national importance. In fact, the central authority's control over municipalities primarily serves to ensure its interests in education, communal economy and other areas.

The opinion that the independence of municipalities is limited only to areas of national importance, and this independence is preserved in purely local affairs, is also unfounded. In the conditions of the current period, not only the control of the central organizations, but also their direct orders are spreading to all spheres of municipal administration.

According to some authors, more and more key decisions are taken by the center, and local representative organizations only have to carry them out. These circumstances turn the local representative organizations into a mechanism for executing the directives of the central government, and they become an outgrowth of the national administration.

In the current period, the reason for the center's intervention in municipal affairs is interpreted as ensuring the same high standards in the management of areas of national importance. But in fact, the central authority's control over municipalities primarily serves to ensure its interests in education, communal economy and other areas.

---

[17] Dual (Eng.) – two-sided or consisting of two parts.

Also, in recent decades, a municipal concept related to the theory of the "general welfare state" has appeared.

Municipalities began to be recognized as a social service institution that provides and protects the interests of all classes of society. The theory of "social service" was also accepted as one of the manifestations of the concept of "general welfare state".

However, the state authorities have started to develop and support municipal services that only serve the interests of large businessmen.

Conflicts began to arise between the needs for housing, education, and social security, and the government's attempt to stimulate the area of municipal activity that is beneficial for private entrepreneurs. Municipal social programs related to housing, healthcare and other areas related to the expansion of private entrepreneurship began to take priority. Accordingly, the material bases of the social functions of local government organizations were shrinking.

In many countries, the concepts of local government standing outside of politics have emerged, according to which municipalities should stand outside of politics, be service- providing apparatuses, and specialize in providing certain services to civil society.

Often, the concept that "municipalities are out of politics" became the basis for banning strikes by municipal employees. Also, efforts are being made to prove the use of activity forms and methods characteristic of private corporations in municipal tets. Municipal councilors feel certain effects of voters. As a result, they are declared as "bad administrators". The main goal of those promoting the apoliticization of municipalities is not to isolate these organizations from political life (which is impossible!), but to try to make them a submissive instrument of government policy.

Thus, the municipal organizations of the modern state are not interpreted as real local self-government organizations. From a socio- political point of view, they have never been able to become a self-governing body of the entire population. On the other hand, considering local self-government as the decisive political-legal quality of these institutions remains a thing of the past for municipalism. If the election of local officials, the lack of appointment of authority from above, the local self in the 19th century served as the main criteria of self-management, while they performed a narrow range of secondary tasks with minimal intervention from the center, but by the middle of the 20th century, the situation had changed dramatically. Although elections and the absence of local agents of the central government retain their importance as elements of municipal democracy, these circumstances do not prevent the center from coordinating municipal activities in all respects.

CONTROL QUESTIONS

1. What is the essence of the activity of self-government (municipal) bodies?
2. What do municipal (self-government) system models include?
3. What are the concepts of the system of municipal (self-government) bodies?

3- THEME: MODERNIZATION OF THE STATE EXECUTIVE POWER SYSTEM: INTERNATIONAL AND UZBEK EXPERIENCE

Plan:

1. Views on state power in Europe in the 17th century.
2. Constitution - modernization of the system of state power as the legal basis
3. "Strategy of Actions" methodological basis of modernization of the State Executive system of Uzbekistan.

Since the emergence of the state and society several thousand years ago in the history of the world, mankind has longed for the state to serve the interests and goals of the society and people, and continuous struggles have continued for this goal. Despite this, the problems of humanity on the way to building a populist state have not been solved. The new era - by the 17th century, the theoretical aspects of curbing the despotism of the state power, ensuring its functioning in the way of the people's well-being and the development of the society began to take shape. This discovery was a theory related to the formation of the principles of dividing state power into three. The first modern ideas about the division of state power into three, the strengthening of one of the branches of power and the prevention of oppression and use of force against society and its members, the popularization of power were the English thinker John Locke (1632-1704) and the French enlightener Charles Louis Montesquieu put forward by, of course, attention was paid to the fact that the government has extremely powerful resources, and if it is allowed to rule the society based on its own will, it will inevitably lead to totalitarianism, oppression of citizens, and deviations from the law.

According to Montesquieu (1689-1775), if the leaders of the society unite in one group and collect the entire reins of power in their hands, there is a danger that revolutions will begin at the initiative of other groups fighting for power, and there will be a danger of their constant repetition. In this process, a group of managers acting on behalf of an entire society becomes a ruling oligarchy, which ultimately loses its creative and developmental character. Montesquieu developed the theoretical foundations of the doctrine of separation of powers and put forward the ideas of mutual "balance" and "restraint" of powers. He also expressed the opinion that it is necessary for state authorities to represent all social classes in the society.[18] The meaning of this word is that it is necessary and necessary for the people to participate in state management through their elected representatives. Important attention was paid to the prevention of negative events such as arbitrariness, artificial increase of powers, violations of human rights and freedoms as a result of strengthening of one of the three branches of government and the weakening of other branches of government.

According to Montesquieu's draft of a constitutional republic, the legislative power is the expression of "the general will of the state". Its main task is to define rights and form them in the form of positive laws that oblige all citizens to fulfill them.

---

[18] See: Montesquieu Sh. O duxe zakonov. – M.: Elektronnoye biblioteka: Graj danskoye obshestvo v Rossii, 2010. – P.147–148, 154–155.

According to the thinker, the legislative and executive authorities, which have a legal character, can abuse power and allow arbitrariness, unlike the judiciary. That is why these two authorities should not only be mutually divided, but one should be provided with the rights to stop and cancel the activity of the other. The executive power should be built as a body that implements the general will of the state. His task is to implement only the laws established by the legislature. Therefore, "executive power should be limited according to its nature", its powers should be given to the monarch. Because "this aspect of administration requires quick action, its powers are better fulfilled by one person than many". The executive power is exercised by people other than members of the legislative assembly.

The result of the interaction of the legislative and executive authorities is a guarantee for the existence of the right, which reconciles the conflicts of wills and interests of different social strata and forces.

The legislature not only makes laws, but also supervises their implementation by the executive, that is, the monarch and his ministers.

The government or its members can be held accountable by the legislature for breaking the law. The executive power takes measures to prevent the legislative power from becoming arbitrariness, has the right to veto the decisions of the legislative power, establishes regulations for the work of the two chambers, and has the right to dissolve them.

S. Montesquieu's ideas on the separation of powers were expressed in the French Constitution adopted in 1791. The following words were written on it: "Authority as a society that has not been divided and is not provided with the right to use it will not have a valid constitution".

Despite the passage of more than two centuries, Montesquieu's theoretical views on the separation of powers are still alive as one of the main principles of the constitutions of developed countries. In the process of gradual development over several centuries, the parliament has developed and improved as a legislative power, as a law-making body, as a supreme representative body, and as the main state body that controls the execution of laws.

True democratic values and the constitutional principles of the separation of powers characteristic of a legal state were formed in Uzbekistan only during the period of independence. Especially with the formation of a two-chamber professional parliament operating on the basis of democratic principles and national interests in the country, the principle of separation of powers began to be implemented at the level of the requirements of the legal state and civil society.

In the next decade, as a result of the gradual transfer of new powers to the parliament, the growth of the legal culture of our people, and the development of political parties based on democratic values, the legislative power embodied in itself the qualities and characteristics typical of modern parliaments. According to Article 78 of the Constitution of the Republic of Uzbekistan, the joint powers of the Legislative Chamber and the Senate are defined as the following: adoption of the Constitution of the Republic of Uzbekistan, amendments and additions to it; adoption of constitutional laws and laws of the Republic of Uzbekistan, amendments and additions to them; Conducting the referendum of the Republic of Uzbekistan making a decision about and setting the date of its holding; Determining the main directions of internal and external policy of the Republic of Uzbekistan and adopting state strategic programs; Determining the system and powers of legislative, executive and judicial authorities of the Republic of Uzbekistan; Accepting new state structures into the Republic of Uzbekistan and approving decisions about their withdrawal from the Republic of Uzbekistan; regulation of customs, currency and credit matters by law; Acceptance of the State budget of the Republic of Uzbekistan and control of its execution, according to the submission of the Cabinet of Ministers of the Republic of Uzbekistan; introduction of taxes and other mandatory payments; Regulation of the issues of the administrative-territorial structure of the Republic of Uzbekistan by law, changing the borders; establishment, termination of districts, cities, regions, changing their names and boundaries; establishment of state awards and titles; Republic of Uzbekistan, Approving decrees of the President on the formation and termination of ministries, state committees and other organizations of state administration; Establishing the Central Election Commission of the Republic of Uzbekistan; Reviewing and approving the candidacy of the Prime Minister of the Republic of Uzbekistan based on the presentation of the President of the Republic of Uzbekistan, as well as hearing and discussing the Prime Minister's reports on current issues of the country's socio-economic development; Electing the representative of the Oliy Majlis of the Republic of Uzbekistan on Human Rights and his deputy; Review of the report of the Accounts Chamber of the Republic of Uzbekistan; Republic of Uzbekistan Approving the decree of the President on the declaration of a state of war in the event of an attack on the Republic of Uzbekistan or in the event of the need to fulfill the contractual obligations concluded on mutual defense against aggression; Proclamation of general or partial mobilization of the President of the Republic of Uzbekistan, introduction of a state of emergency, and its implementation, approval of decrees on extension or termination; ratification and denunciation of international agreements.

Article 79 of the Constitution defines the following as absolute powers of the Legislative Chamber: electing the Speaker of the Legislative Chamber of the Oliy Majlis of the Republic of Uzbekistan and his deputies, chairmen of committees and their deputies; To resolve the issues of depriving a deputy of the Legislative Chamber of the Oliy Majlis of the Republic of Uzbekistan of the right to immunity based on the presentation of the Prosecutor General of the Republic of Uzbekistan; making decisions on issues related to the organization of its activities and internal procedures of the chamber; It includes making decisions on one or another issue in the field of political, socio- economic life, as well as on issues of internal and foreign policy of the state.

Article 80 of the Constitution defines the following as the absolute powers of the Senate: to elect the Chairman of the Senate of the Oliy Majlis of the Republic of Uzbekistan and his deputies, the chairmen of the committees and their deputies; Election of the Constitutional Court of the Republic of Uzbekistan on the recommendation of the President of the Republic of Uzbekistan; Electing the Supreme Court of the Republic of Uzbekistan on the recommendation of the President of the Republic of Uzbekistan; To elect the Supreme Economic Court of the Republic of Uzbekistan on the recommendation of the President of the Republic of Uzbekistan; To appoint and dismiss the chairman of the State Committee for Nature Protection of the Republic of Uzbekistan on the recommendation of the President of the Republic of Uzbekistan; Approving decrees of the President of the Republic of Uzbekistan on the appointment and dismissal of the Prosecutor General of the Republic of Uzbekistan and the Chairman of the Accounts Chamber; Republic of Uzbekistan of the President of the Republic of approving decrees appointing and dismissing the chairman of the National Security Service; appoint diplomatic and other representatives of the Republic of Uzbekistan Res publication in foreign countries and release them from their positions on the recommendation of the President of the Republic of Uzbekistan; Appointing and dismissing the chairman of the board of the Central Bank of Publications of Uzbekistan Res according to the recommendation of the President of the Republic of Uzbekistan; Acceptance of amnesty documents upon submission of the President of the Republic of Uzbekistan; To resolve the issues of depriving a member of the Senate of the Oliy Majlis of the Republic of Uzbekistan of the right to immunity based on the presentation of the Prosecutor General of the Republic of Uzbekistan; hearing the reports of the Prosecutor General of the Republic of Uzbekistan, the chairman of the State Committee for Nature Protection of the Republic of Uzbekistan, the chairman of the board of the Central Bank of the Republic of Uzbekistan; making decisions on issues related to the organization of its activities and internal procedures of the chamber; It includes making decisions on one or another issue in the field of political, socio-economic life, as well as on issues of internal and external state policy.

By the present time, the legislative authority of the country has begun to function at a level that meets the requirements of the legal state. As a result of the formation of the qualities and characteristics of the civil society and the legal state, although the legislative process has become more complicated, the quality of the adopted laws has increased. The role of political parties and their parliamentary factions in the adoption of laws has increased. The practice of preliminary review of draft laws in party factions, taking into account the opinions of these factions during the discussion of draft legal documents at plenary sessions of the Legislative Chamber was formed.

Pursuant to Article 5 of the Law of the Republic of Uzbekistan "On Parliamentary Control", which came into force on April 11, 2016, the following forms of parliamentary control were established in the country: the State budget of the Republic of Uzbekistan for the next year, the budgets of state special funds and the main directions of tax and budget policy (hereinafter referred to as the State budget) adoption, as well as reviewing the progress of the State budget execution; Reviewing the annual report of the Cabinet of Ministers of the Republic of Uzbekistan (hereinafter referred to as the Cabinet of Ministers) on the most important issues of the country's socio-economic life; Hearing the report of the Prime Minister of Uzbekistan (hereinafter referred to as the Prime Minister) on some current issues of the socio-economic development of the country; Hearing information from members of the government on issues related to their activities at the meetings of the Legislative Chamber and the Senate; hearing the report of the Accounts Chamber of the Republic of Uzbekistan (hereinafter referred to as the Accounts Chamber); hearing the report of the Prosecutor General of the Republic of Uzbekistan; hearing the report of the chairman of the State Committee for the Protection of Wild Horses of the Republic of Uzbekistan; hearing the

report of the Chairman of the Board of the Central Bank of the Republic of Uzbekistan; parliamentary inquiry; Request of a deputy of the Legislative Chamber, a member of the Senate; hearing the information of the heads of state power and management organizations by the committees of the Legislative Chamber and the Senate; to study the state of execution of legal documents, the practice of applying the law by the committees of the Legislative Chamber, the Senate, and to carry out monitoring by them in connection with the adoption of legal documents; parliamentary scrutiny.

The growth and weight of the control rights granted to the parliament shows that the country needs a modern and professional body that is able to exercise both supreme representation, lawmaking and parliamentary control at the same time. National legislative power - the national parliament was formed.

The Parliament not only has the capacity to easily control the activities of the government and its organizations regarding the execution of laws and the state budget, but also has reached the level of ensuring that the society lives in compliance with the constitutional legal framework and laws.

In the last quarter of 2016, the election of Shavkat Mir Ziyoyev as the President of the country, having achieved the absolute highest level of votes in the Presidential election, was manifested as an important historical reality. Within a short period of half a year, a number of legal frameworks were adopted in the country for the modernization of state supervision, the deepening of reforms of civil society and the establishment of a legal state. They began to be rapidly introduced into socio- political and economic life.

"In-depth analysis of the path of development of our country to the present time requires comprehensive consideration of the fact that today the world market is changing and competition is intensifying, and on this basis, to develop and implement completely new strategic approaches and principles for the development of our country at a more stable and rapid pace." 2017-2021 of the President of the Republic of Uzbekistan The adoption of the decree "On the strategy of actions for the further development of the publication of the Republic of Uzbekistan" for the next few years has started a new stage in the development of civil society in the country.

It contains the Strategy of Actions on the five priority areas of development of the Republic of Uzbekistan within five years (hereinafter referred to as the Strategy of Actions) and the first of them represents the programmatic tasks of the priority areas of improvement of the system of state and society construction.

In the action strategy, the tasks of "increasing the role of the Oliy Majlis in the system of state power, solving important tasks related to the country's internal and foreign policy, and further expanding its powers to implement parliamentary control over the activities of the executive power" were set.

These tasks were focused on strengthening the role of Oliy Majlis chambers and political parties in the modernization of the country.

As an initial task, the Oliy Majlis should ensure mutual balance and mutual restraint with other branches of government based on the principle of separation of powers, and increase its participation in state management. Development of a draft law of the Republic, in which a deputy of the

Legislative Chamber of the Oliy Majlis and a member of the Senate study and analyze the activities of local state authorities as a form of parliamentary control and take appropriate measures based on its results, a representative of the Oliy Majlis for the protection of the rights and legal interests of business entities (determination of the status of the business ombudsman) (hereinafter - the business ombudsman) as a subject of parliamentary control was shown.

In the action strategy, President Shavkat Mirziyoyev put forward the programmatic goals for the implementation of the principle: "The people should serve our people, not the state agencies, and the state agencies should serve our people" in social and political life. That is why the Councils of the Chambers of the Oliy Majlis on the fundamental improvement of the activities of the Legislative Chamber and the Senate of the Oliy Majlis of the Republic of Uzbekistan study the situation on the ground and communicate with the people, legal grounds for developing a draft of a joint resolution, in which the deputies and senators elected from the regions will spend 10-12 days in the same district every month, study and analyze the activities of state authorities, include the report of the relevant leaders in the discussion of the session of the Councils of People's Deputies, and give relevant conclusions was indicated It was also envisaged to hold sessions of relevant Councils of People's Deputies with the participation of the Speaker of the Legislative Chamber and the Chairman of the Senate, and to organize the work of model Councils of People's Deputies in each region by the Senate of the Oliy Majlis.

If we consider that the functioning of the parliament based on the will and interests of the people and the adoption of laws is one of the most basic democratic values inherent in the rule of law, the interaction of the deputies and members of the Senate with their constituents, their awareness of local problems, and their personal participation in finding solutions , supporting the revitalization of local representative organizations creates conditions for the development of the environment and elements of civil society in our country. Because the deputy of the higher representative body is, first of all, the representative of the citizens of his constituency. A member of the Senate is a representative of local representative organizations of the region from which he was elected. That is why the more activities of the members of the parliament among the people will allow them to know the interests of the people and local problems in depth, to bring them into the processes of the parliament, and ultimately, such activities will ensure the stability and peace of our country and our nation as a whole.

In the strategy of actions, development of the draft law of the Republic of Uzbekistan "On the representative of the Oliy Majlis of the Republic of Uzbekistan on the protection of the rights and legal interests of business entities (business ombudsman)", in which the newly established ombudsman will have the following: it was envisaged to grant powers: participation in the formation and implementation of state policy in the field of development of business activities, protection of the rights and legal interests of business entities; legal support of business entities when their activities are being investigated; to study whether the norms and requirements of legal documents on guarantees of freedom of entrepreneurial activity are being implemented in practice; assessment of the effectiveness of the impact of the adopted regulatory legal documents on the implementation of business activities; implementation of control over compliance with the rights and legal interests of business entities by state organizations, law enforcement and control organizations, as well as local government organizations.

The main purpose of establishing a business ombudsman is to comply with laws in the field of protection of legal rights and interests of business entities in the country and the Decree of the President of the Republic of Uzbekistan on October 5, 2016 "Ensuring the rapid development of business activities, comprehensive protection of private property and improving the quality of the business environment" "Additional Measures" is to exercise parliamentary control over the execution of the Decree on It is also envisaged that the business ombudsman will act as the main institution of protection and provision of the economic rights of the citizens of the country, a right inherent in every civil society.

It is clear that the rights and powers granted to the business ombudsman create conditions for the full realization of the labor potential, perseverance, hard work and enthusiasm of entrepreneurs and farmers, the basis of the country's economy. Protection of the class of owners by means of such legal frameworks and institutions, laying the foundation for a separate state policy to ensure their rights and freedoms - this is the developed countries of our country. It means that it is striving towards a legal state.

Because the class of owners is the economic base and social support of civil society. In the strategy of actions, development of the draft law of the Republic of Uzbekistan "On Amendments and Additions to the Law of the Republic of Uzbekistan "On Human Rights Representative (Ombudsman) of the Oliy Majlis of the Republic of Uzbekistan", in which the norms of this law "On Appeals of Natural and Legal Entities", " Alignment with the laws "On the openness of the activities of state authorities and management organizations", "On social partnership", "On parliamentary control" and defining the legal status, powers and obligations of the regional representatives of the ombudsman.

The promotion of these strategic tasks is based on the Citizens' Reception of the Office of the President of the Republic of Uzbekistan in accordance with the Decree of the President of the Republic of Uzbekistan "On measures to fundamentally improve the system of working with appeals of natural and legal entities" adopted on December 28, 2016. People's Reception of the President of the Republic of Uzbekistan, People's Reception of the President of the Republic of Uzbekistan (hereinafter - public reception) and the virtual reception of the President of the Republic of Uzbekistan (hereinafter - public reception) established in the Republic of Karakalpakstan, regions and the city of Tosh Kent, as well as in each district and city (except cities subordinate to the district) - Virtual reception) is inextricably linked with the determination of tasks and powers.

According to the Presidential Decree, it is necessary to organize their direct contact with the population, the rights of individuals and legal entities and focused on the full protection of their freedoms and legal interests.

According to it, the following directions of legal protection are formed: ensuring the operation of a qualitatively new and efficient system of working with appeals of individuals and legal entities (hereinafter referred to as appeals); appeal of citizens to the President of the Republic of Uzbekistan, the Oliy Majlis, the Office of the President of the Republic of Uzbekistan, the Government, state administration organizations, courts, law enforcement and control organizations, local state authorities, other state organizations (hereinafter - state organizations) and economic management organizations create conditions for the unconditional realization of their constitutional rights; Implementation of systematic monitoring and control over consideration of appeals sent to public receptions and Virtual receptions, as well as those sent to state organizations and economic management organizations; Tasks such as introducing and maintaining a single electronic information system for monitoring, recording, summarizing, systematizing and reviewing appeals received at public receptions and Virtual receptions, as well as wide use of modern information and communication technologies in working with appeals have been defined.

At the same time, with the adoption of the laws "On the openness of the activities of state authorities and management organizations", "On social partnership", and "On parliamentary control", the implementation of parliamentary control in the country has been brought to the level typical of civil society and the rule of law. raising has become an urgent task.

That is why the Oliy Majlis representative on human rights (Ombudsman) is given a number of powers to bring the processes of implementation of the laws contained in the above- mentioned laws and the processes of ensuring their transparency under the control of the parliament, to protect citizens' legal rights and freely creates opportunities to resolve appeals regarding violations in a fair and efficient manner. The rights of the Human Rights Representative (Ombudsman) of the Oliy Majlis, which carries out the activities of the Parliament on the protection and provision of human rights and freedoms, will be raised to the level of international standards and its functioning as an independent institution is guaranteed.

Development of the draft law of the Republic of Uzbekistan on increasing the role and position of the chambers of the Oliy Majlis in the implementation of the state's foreign policy in the strategy of actions, in which the control powers of the chambers of the Oliy Majlis in the implementation of the state's foreign policy, their control over the implementation of international law norms into national legislation, the parliaments of foreign countries with the objectives of improving the legal mechanisms for organizing the work of inter- parliamentary cooperation groups, expanding the possibilities of wide use of parliamentary diplomacy in the realization of the country's national interests, and further improvement of their legal foundations was envisaged. As a result of the adoption of this law, the prospects for further democratization of the foreign policy of our country, comprehensive cooperation with the countries of the world in ensuring peace and stability, development of the legal foundations of processes such as expressing national interests in the international arena, deeper penetration into world integration, and increasing the role of the parliament in this field have been determined.

In the action strategy, it was determined to develop a comprehensive program of measures for the introduction of the "Electronic Parliament" system in order to improve the interaction of the population with senators and deputies, and the communication of the Oliy Majlis with the people, and to prepare a draft of the decision of the President of the Republic of

Uzbekistan on its adoption. In this draft decision, it is planned to implement the following tasks: increase the efficiency and transparency of the work of the nation striving to improve communication with the people through the wide introduction of information and communication technologies to the activities of the parliament; to send to the deputies the decisions of the local authorities where their constituencies are located; to create an opportunity to be constantly aware of the situation in this area.

The development of the "Electronic Parliament" system will increase the role of the parliament in the implementation of the principle of separation of powers in our country, it will further strengthen the interactions and relations of the parliament with the citizens of the electoral districts, local representative organizations, and create conditions for the further development of the electronic cooperation system with them. This system provides uniform technological approaches to the formation of this system, which provides a mechanism for the design, development and integration of the database and information resources used in the parliamentary chambers. It can be seen that the "Electronic Parliament" system is far from fulfilling the role of modern information communication that connects the mutual relations between the parliamentary chambers and citizens, it is an institution that carries various interests of citizens to the process of drafting laws and represents these interests in the parliament. In turn, it is inevitable that these processes will have a strong influence on the social and political activation of citizens. Of course, in this process, one of the main components of socialization of citizens - the legal and political culture of citizens - also inc In the action strategy, the task of developing the draft Law of the Republic of Uzbekistan "On Amendments and Additions to the Law of the Republic of Uzbekistan "On Political Parties" aimed at expanding the rights and powers of political party deputation groups to exercise control over the activities of local executive organizations was set. This draft law emorganizations the following legal frameworks: consideration of socio-economic development issues by party groups at the sessions of local councils of people's deputies; to introduce a proposal to hear the reports of officials of local executive authorities; submit the district (city) mayor's candidate to the district (city) Council of People's Deputies for approval after consultations with each of the party groups in the relevant Councils of People's Deputies; to give party groups in the local Councils of People's Deputies the right to present conclusions about the unsatisfactory performance of district (city) hokims, as well as heads of local executive organizations, in relation to the hokims of the regions and Tashkent city; To attach representatives of regional branches of the relevant political party to the deputies of the Legislative Chamber as representatives of the electorate in the electoral districts of the regions.

These tasks in the action strategy are based on the scheme "voters (citizens) - political parties - political party factions in the parliament (party groups in local representative organizations) - laws, regulatory documents, decisions of state organizations" in the country, the interests and wills of citizens, state power, including The development of democratic processes, such as expression in the activities of local authorities, their reflection in laws and decisions of authorities, has a positive effect on the economy. In other words, local representative and executive organizations appear as organizations that operate based on the interests of the people.

On the basis of the action strategy, it is assumed that the granting of new rights and powers to party groups will lead to the following socio-political changes: further strengthening of the activities of local representative organizations; in this regard, creating conditions for increasing the role of local deputies in society through political parties; activation of party groups formed in local representative organizations; ensure that they become an organizationally effective force; raising problems in the area, revitalizing their activities to find solutions. In particular, giving importance to the fact that the center of competition between political parties takes place between party groups, discussions and debates between different programmatic and ideological goals ensures the growth of pluralistic ideological views of the population, the diversity of multi-party and ideological views characteristic of civil society, and the conflicts between them. reconciliation creates conditions for ensuring the mobilization of the population towards common goals.

Further improvement of regulatory documents, which harmonize the mutual relations of party groups in local representative organizations, create conditions for these relations to have a positive effect on the economic and social development of local regions, in the interests of citizens representation and protection through local representative organizations enriches their imaginations and views about children, increases their social activities.

In the action strategy, establishment of the position of the Permanent Representative of the Cabinet of Ministers in the Oliy Majlis Chambers (hereinafter - Permanent Representative), whose permanent task is to increase the effectiveness of mutual cooperation of the legislative and executive authorities in the field of law-making, as well as in the organization of parliamentary control over the activities of the executive authority focus is set. Such a permanent representative institution of the government is showing itself as a special link in strengthening the interaction between the parliament and the government in all developed countries. Parliamentary activity and law-making of the permanent representative as the representatives

Being aware of all the details of the processes, participation in the formation of drafts of regulatory legal documents creates opportunities to increase the efficiency of the adopted laws, to adapt them to new conditions that arise, as well as to increase the role of the executive power in improving the draft of laws, to implement parliamentary control over the implementation of laws. will further improve, quickly establish relations between the government and the parliament, ensure that the laws are popular, mature and thorough.

Modernization of the state power system first began in the 17th century in England, France and the Netherlands.

One of the characteristics of modernized societies is the development of civil society and legal state or their elements.

Decentralization reforms, which formed the basis of administrative reforms, began in France, Great Britain, Germany and Sweden in the 1980s and 1990s. By the end of the 20th century, these processes began in all countries of Europe and North America. However, by the present time, state reforms in most countries, no matter which of the administrative, budgetary and state management directions are implemented, are focused on the implementation of the following goals, which are common to all of them: improving the quality of the budget service; increase the efficiency of public spending; improving the quality of the activity and management system of the executive power and its organizations at all levels.

In Western countries, self-governing (municipal) organizations functioned as a political organization performing lower local government functions several centuries ago, but by the 20th century, they became an institution of civil society, and municipal government became a relatively insignificant form of state government. At the same time, it began to function as an institution of civil society.

The main characteristics of such governing organizations are their election and relative independence in managing matters of local importance based on the interests of the population in their territory.

During the 19th and 20th centuries, three models of interaction between the center and local self-government organizations were formed (English, French and Prussian). Today, models based on these established traditions - Anglo-Saxon, French (or southern European model) and Germanic (or northern - Central European model) are still in use in life.

The most exemplary of local self-government is the Anglo- Saxon model, in which the processes of self-government take place "within the local interests of the authorities". In the French model of self-government, power is (formally) in the hands of local government organizations that oversee self-government. In the German model, state administration and local self-government are combined as a single institution.

Reforms to modernize local and self-governing organizations in Western countries were carried out under the influence of the following conditions: a) in the context of the dominance of national governments; b) as a result of attempts to take mass actions on the ground (for example, such as a wave of widespread protests); d) As in the USA, most political subjects are in a state of mutual solidarity or equal rights for all, as well as the absence of clearly expressed participation of the center. At the same time, in the course of reforms in this field, elements of civil society began to form.

One of the principles of the enlargement of municipal organizations in the West was to give additional powers to newly created organizations (in France to regions, in the USA to metropolitan councils). In addition, many public service functions are devolved directly to local authorities or their agencies without any intermediate management links.

From the given point of view of national governments, these reforms were seen as implementation of decentralization.

In addition, the following requirements were imposed on local self-government organizations: the ability to meet the needs of citizens; a means of meeting the needs of citizens; the legitimacy of his leadership in his community; ability to adapt to changes in society; freedom to be influenced by local conditions in relation to the specific needs and demands of their community.

In most Western countries, municipal councils are legally above the management of the municipal apparatus, and their powers include: adopting the local budget, making normative decisions on certain issues that are within their jurisdiction and not resolved by higher organizations, introducing local taxes, borrowing and solving the issues of their use, disposal of property belonging to the municipality, establishment of executive management organizations of the municipality in most countries and their control, setting of local referendums.

Municipalities began to occupy an important place in the life of the USA. Because the principle of decentralization of municipal functions is widely used in them. Management of municipal schools, hospitals, libraries, sanitation, water supply, parks, and fire services is in most cases the responsibility of municipal councils, which are carried out through special districts. Elected or appointed organizations of special districts: management, committees, etc.

They are closely related to the state administration and are not subject to municipal councils. It is often observed that executive organizations take over the functions of municipal councils. In some countries, municipal councils have the right to delegate their powers to executive organizations.

From the beginning of President Shavkat Mirziyoyev's work as the head of state in Uzbekistan, a national model of state administration and service modernization was developed based on the combination of developed countries and national experience. The "Strategy of Actions for Further Development of the Republic of Uzbekistan" and "Concept of Administrative Reforms in Uzbekistan" developed at the initiative of President Shavkat Mirziyoyev have emerged as the main methodological basis for the modernization of public administration and service and the formation of The implementation of the conceptual goals aimed at increasing the role of the parliament in the separation of powers defined in the action strategy will directly prepare the ground for the adoption of laws taking into account the interests and will of the people, the activation of the participation of citizens in the activities of state authorities, and the priority directions of the activities of these organizations will increase the well-being of the people.

Also, this process of changes is manifested as the legal basis for the development of socio-political, legal and intellectual relations characteristic of civil society and the legal state. Of course, the implementation of these changes, further democratization of society, representation of people's interests in the activities of state authorities, in turn, will inevitably have a positive effect on the development of market economy relations and the further growth of the country's economic potential.

CONTROL QUESTIONS

1. What are the views of state power in Europe in the 17th century?
2. What does the Constitution include as a legal basis for the modernization of the state power system?
3. "Strategy of actions" - what is the methodological basis of modernization of the system of state executive power of Uzbekistan?

4-THEME: THE PROCESS OF MODERNIZATION OF THE STATE EXECUTIVE POWER SYSTEM IN ANGLO-SAXON COUNTRIES

Plan:

1. The experience of modernization of British public authorities
2. State power fundamental changes in the field of modernization in Great Britain at the beginning of the 21st century
3. The experience of modernization of US state authorities

The current two-party system in Great Britain dates back to the late 17th century when the Tory and Whig parties formed. Since the beginning of the First World War, the Conservative and Labor parties have been taking turns in the government, gaining the trust of the voters. In terms of form of government, Great Britain is a parliamentary republic. This form of government has existed since the 9th century.

In English public legal doctrine, the monarch is the first in the system of state organizations and is the source of sovereign power. Great Britain has the Castilian system of succession, which means that the eldest son or daughter of the monarch inherits the throne. Elizabeth II has been on the throne since 1952.

The Monarch, the House of Commons and the House of Lords are part of the Parliament. The lower house - the general house - is a national representative, is a body and is elected for 5 years. The lower house is headed by the speaker, who is the leader of the house. The Speaker is elected by the House until his term expires and he must not belong to any party. Bills are considered by the lower house and submitted to the upper house.

The Lord Chancellor presides over the House of Lords. At the same time, the parliament controls the activities of the ministers. The two Houses may jointly form joint committees to deal with tasks related to the work of each House. Deputies enjoy the right of immunity.

The judicial power of the English Parliament is exercised by the House of Lords.

The UK government has a somewhat unique system. The composition of the cabinet and the official government do not match. The cabinet exists only by constitutional convention (there is no law governing the legal status of the government or the cabinet). Ministers are appointed by cabinet members. The government is headed by the prime minister, and the old government consists of 20-22 ministers. They include the Lord Chancellor, the Chancellor of the Exchequer, the Secretaries of State for Home Affairs and Defence, as well as other ministers. The composition of the cabinet is as varied as the composition of the government. Close and trusted members of the Prime Minister's cabinet (3-5 people) enter the "inner cabinet". Decisions made by them (in rare cases, the cabinet meeting is convened in full composition) are later formalized on behalf of the entire cabinet.

In necessary situations, the number and people of the members of the "inner cabinet" can be changed by the prime minister.

The government is usually formed by the prime minister from the ruling party's deputies (about 100). It includes four groups of ministers. The first is the heads of individual ministries. Some of them, that is, those who occupy leading positions, enter the cabinet.

The rest of the ministers are based on the decisions made by the cabinet depending on the activity of the ministry they manage (if the cabinet did not offer it) are accepted.

The second group consists of ministers without portfolios and members of the government working in various traditional positions. These are, for example, the lord chairman of the ken gash, the lord keeper of the seal, and others. In each specific government, the prime minister assigns them special duties. Ministers of the third group are called state ministers - they are deputy ministers of major ministries. The fourth group is junior ministers, who are parliamentary secretaries who liaise between ministers and parliament. The change in the relationship with the parliament, the complexity of the government's management task and the conflict of ideas with the large armed forces (army) required the revival of the last two groups of ministers. In 1986, there were three ministers of state, and one and a half times more parliamentary secretaries than cabinet members.

One of the main directions of the government is to manage the complex state apparatus. He plays a decisive role not only in appointment, but also in changing positions and dismissal. Through ministries, departments, headquarters and other organizations, the government implements the will of the state.

As the government is an executive body, it is obliged to implement the laws passed by the parliament. Law enforcement leads to government's own rule-making activities. Controlling the legislative activity of the Parliament has become one of the main directions of the government's activity.

The local government of the state includes Wales, Scotland, Northern Ireland and, in particular, England itself. Some of the ethnic groups differ from each other in terms of their national composition, language, and level of socio-economic development. The Isle of Man and the Isle of Wight are part of Great Britain. They also have their own legislatures. Their laws come into force after receiving the Queen's sanction. Defense stability in international relations is carried out by the UK government.

The Local Government Act of 1972 established a two-tier system of local government. The territory of England and Wales is divided into counties (39 in England, 8 in Wales). Counties are divided into counties (339 of which

296 are in England, 37 are in Wales, 26 are in Northern Ireland). 6 large cities have received the status of metropolitan counties. In 1975, 9 regions were formed in Scotland, and 53 counties were formed in them.

A decentralized local government system was formed in Great Britain. The lowest level of local government is pri hods (communities in Wales). Their number reached 11 thousand. If the population of prikhod is less than 150 voters, decisions are made at the general meeting of all residents. Councils are formed by direct elections for a 4-year term and include a chairman and advisers. The chairman is re-elected by the councilors every year, and one-third of the councilors are also re-elected every year. These organizations are involved in police management, firefighting, road service, museum work, social services, and care for the elderly.

From the 80s of the 20th century, the experience of modernization of public authorities of Great Britain served as a model for other countries. In Great Britain, the culture of civil society and representation of local interests in representative organizations is at the forefront. In the field of administrative management, 2 models of it were formed: "partnership" and "agency"1. In the "partnership" model, local authorities have been given greater independence in defining and implementing their own policies. Although they are under the control of the parliament, they are not equal to other central organizations got a lot. In the "Agency" model, the local self-governing organizations, which have achieved the status of greater independence, were provided with the powers to implement the national policy. The transfer of powers of the central authorities to lower-level authorities (devolution) has become one of the great realities in the British political system.

In the second half of the 20th century, the autonomy of the local authorities was more limited, their accountability to the central government increased, and the priority of the agency model compared to the partnership model began to appear along with the growth of the central government control. Therefore, the researchers compared the results of reforms in this area of Great Britain with European countries and noted that its administrative and management system is relatively centralized.1 The government of Great Britain greatly limited the autonomy of local regions while other European countries are deepening the decentralization of management. Within the framework of such principles, there was a need to significantly increase the efficiency and social importance of the administrative-management system.

According to the researchers, at the end of the 20th century, the pattern2 that is characteristic of the current British local government and was put into new forms emerged. Political scientist M. Lafl in describes it as follows:

1) multi-functionality as responsibility for a wide range of services, important for the general well-being of the state;

2) multi-management participation to create broad collective opportunities for effective problem solving the experience of operation of separate management organizations on the basis of connection to wide networks was formed.

By the beginning of the 21st century, the effectiveness of the local government system has increased. It can be expressed in the following descriptive terms: 1) the formation of the ability of local authorities to coordinate any management functions, as well as having the opportunity to choose a strategy for the well-being and development of local areas; 2) that local authorities have become the only agency representing the interests of local territorial structures at the national level.

At the beginning of the 21st century, fundamental changes were made in the field of modernization of state power in Great Britain.

Dramatic changes have taken place in this country, which has long been regarded as a conservative country in the field of public administration reform. This period of fundamental changes can be divided into three stages:

- neoconservative reforms (M. Thatcher 1979-1990, Dj. Major 1990-1997);
- Labor reforms (T. Blair 1997-2007, G. Brown 2007-2010);
- the second wave of neoconservative reforms (D. Ke meron 2010 - 2016).

At the beginning of the 80s of the 20th century, during the time of Margaret Thatcher, who headed the state administration as the Prime Minister, market economy principles were introduced into the state administration system, and this system entered into competition with the administration in the private sector. In this new approach, priority was given mainly to the reduction of the bureaucratic apparatus, while at the same time, the development of the initiative tendencies of the bureaucracy and the acquisition of the ability to control the social development were given priority.

First, state property was privatized and given to private individuals. In 1992, the Ministry of Energy was abolished and nationalized energy companies were sold to private individuals. However, as a result of these reforms, the results of the monopolistic approach to the management of the population in the state administration did not bring the anticipated benefit to the consumers of the administration service.

The government evaluated the public service sector of the state based on certain values and held competitive tenders2 to give it to the private sector. The central and local organizations of the authorities envisaged the performance of various services from such trade contests, such as guarding, beautification and beautification of service buildings, cleaning the streets of cities and villages from waste.

As a result of this, changes took place in the activities of public administration institutions: companies that provide direct services to the population were created in the structure of most departments3, and they began to operate on the basis of contractual relations with the departments. In addition, market relations were introduced into the system of state institutions. As a result, the state government has the ability to independently use the state budget and allocate resources.

Another introduction of new market relations into public administration was the use of transfers and vouchers.

As a result of the inclusion of the child in education, local education departments lost the right to determine which school a child should attend. In this way, students and their parents decide for themselves which university or school to spend their vouchers on.

In order to improve the efficiency of public administration, the program "Inspection of efficiency" was developed. This program led to a dramatic shift in the implementation of departmental spending audits. The inspection method called "Reiner1 questionnaires" had several goals: to eliminate the duplication of work of departments, increase the efficiency of management services and reduce its costs; identify the losses of each department - lost opportunities, develop guidelines for civil service reform. The general report on the results of the inspection will include recommendations for the implementation of changes and opportunities for improvement of the work while recording the current situation.

The requests to civil servants ranged from social service payments to increased vigilance in security services. According to the researchers, this method of inspection fully justified itself in practice and saved 2 billion pounds from the budget.

Another important reform in public administration was the implementation of MINIS (Management Information System for Ministers). This program focused on identifying many management issues, namely: What happened? Who is responsible for this?

What were the goals? Has monitoring been done for this work? etc. The continuation of the reforms is the "Financial Supervisory Initiative" (FMI) - all central management institutions focused on making fundamental changes in Its main goal is for managers of any level to know in detail the task they have set for themselves and to feel in advance how their work results will be evaluated by means of the formation of new systems in each ministry; his personal responsibility for effective use of resources; Has he received the necessary information, advice, and acquired the necessary education to effectively fulfill his obligations?

The main goal of the program was to try to decentralize state administration: to transfer responsibility for the correct use of budget funds to lower organizations, to create special centers that receive reports on budget expenditures of leaders.

As a result of the activity of these centers, the traditional management methods of the centralized bureaucratic apparatus began to be abolished.

On the initiative of Prime Minister M. Thatcher, in 1987, a new reform program - "Next Steps" was developed.

The name of this reform is taken from the report "Improving Government Management: The Next Steps" by the Department of Efficiency of the Ministry of Finance. Key findings of this report focused on future reforms, some of which included:

- most civil servants retired from government services;

-       in the top management of the government, there are many officials who have acquired knowledge and skills in the implementation of state-level political management, and they have not acquired effective experience of providing public management services;
-       due to the fact that the amount of civil service has increased, and its composition varies from region to region, it is difficult to implement effective management as a whole.

The report sets out new challenges - a whole new way of running the public service.

First of all, it was envisaged to create special executive agencies independent of the central administration to provide specific services to the population. These same agencies were supposed to take over three-fourths of the public service. At the same time, the political powers of ministerial advisers and the duties of officials were separated from each other.

The agency was headed by the chief executive director, who was directly responsible to the minister, from whom he received planning tasks related to the sale of services to the population. But at the same time, he was provided with management and financial freedoms to carry out his work effectively. The tasks of such agencies have become more general: to provide services to the public quickly and in a timely manner in a way that increases the quality and efficiency. The regulations of the principles of general supervision stipulate the following: the agency rewards its specialists based on the results of their professional activity; provides employees with the autonomy and powers necessary for their work; provide them with support services to improve their work; they are encouraged to discover new things and quickly adapt to changes; a balance between service standards and the need to meet local needs is ensured; ways to save money and improve service delivery, including information technology systems, will be developed.

"Next steps" reforms have spread widely in the country.

In its framework, networks of various executive agencies have spread widely: their number has reached 100, and 400,000 employees work in these agencies. In particular, in Australia, the amount of funds specified in the contracts of the government with such private agencies, which have adopted this experience, is a quarter of the funds spent on the entire state apparatus, started to organize one.

The "Citizens' Charter" program adopted by the government in 1991 fundamentally changed the relationship between government agencies and the population. The main task of the reforms based on this program was to increase the effectiveness of the administration among the population by providing communal and other social services to the population. The main principles of the charter were as follows:

1) setting standards - the expected expectations of users of public services - setting certain standards of service in a clear and unambiguous manner, defining and announcing them;

2) to publicly announce practical instructions obtained in a manner compared to the standards;

3) transparency - providing complete and accurate information to the population quickly and without any obstacles. In this case, communal and social service works, their prices, managers of these services should be conveniently delivered to everyone;

4) providing advice - constantly and regularly studying the needs of consumers of social services. It is necessary to take into account the opinion of the population about the provision of services when making additions to the standards;

5) politeness - the requirement to treat the population with courtesy. Services are provided equally and equally to all persons entitled to receive them; services should be provided in convenient ways for consumers. Civil servants must wear badges with their name on their chests;

6) complaints - if any inappropriate behavior occurs in the provision of services, immediately apologize to the consumer, provide information about the incident, quickly find effective means to correct deficiencies;

7) productivity - striving to find effective and low-cost ways of providing services to the population; to confirm and honestly verify that the services specified by the standards are mutually exclusive.

In Great Britain, the "Market Testing" program, adopted in 1992, played an important role in the reform of public administration. The government adopted the document "Competition for Quality", which defined the following main directions of reforms:

- expansion of service areas provided to private entities on the basis of competitions;
- to determine the promising directions of such contracted services (for example, execution of clerical work, services in the field of information, etc.);
– Contractors in relation to VAT (value added tax). eliminating the factors that hinder the initiative;

- payment of labor as a result of the return of the spent funds and the justification of quality indicators of service.

Public administration in its own way needed to be tested by the market, and it was connected with giving the powers of administrative institutions to private contractors on the basis of contests. It focused on the following: in any case, testing through the market ensures reimbursement of costs.

According to the researchers, the reason for the successful implementation of public administration reforms in Great Britain is that another reform was carried out along with the introduction of innovations into the system of authorities, that is, the control of the state apparatus, as well as over it, was seriously strengthened.2 In 1992-1993, the audit service was completely was reformed, the inspectorate, audit and other control services were expanded, and they acquired the character of regularity in announcing their inspection activities and results. In general, the neocon reforms have significantly changed the face of the British system of government.

When Labor (led by Tony Blair) came to power, reforms began in the legislative and judicial structures of public administration. Initially, the parliament was reformed by ending the principle of succession (membership in the House of Lords was inherited from generation to generation). In March 2007, the House of Lords ruled against the Prime Minister's proposal, but the reform did not come to fruition.

In 2003, a constitutional reform was carried out. According to him, the position of the Lord Chancellor of Great Britain was terminated.

After that, the judicial system, which ruled for 800 years, was thoroughly reformed. The Lord Chancellor was simultaneously the head of the judiciary (he appointed all the courts), the Speaker of the Upper House of Parliament, and a member of the Cabinet. In the new state system, instead of the position of the Lord Chancellor, 4 institutions were established individually: 1) the Supreme Court of Great Britain as the highest court instance; 2) the right to appoint courts was given to a special and independent commission for appointing courts; 3) the upper chamber of the parliament had the right to elect its chairman; 4) a new position of minister responsible for constitutional affairs was established within the government.

In short, Great Britain's transition from a monarchy to a democratic state has reached its end.

Under Prime Minister Gordon Brown, a proposal was made to adopt a formal UK constitution. Work in this area began in 2007, but until now, its results have not been seen. But he managed to create a new authority - the National Security Council. This state body is aimed at solving national security problems during crises.

David Cameron, who came to power in 2010, initiated a new wave of modernization of public authorities. During this period, the government reduced spending, raised taxes and implemented some of the largest social welfare, health, education, and police reforms since World War II.

In essence, these reforms were evaluated as the reconstruction of the welfare state. In the reforms, much attention was paid to the distribution of material wealth based on the principles of social justice and equalization of the living standards of different social groups.

In conclusion, Great Britain, which developed in the 20th century under very conservative views, implemented modern administrative reforms, the main core of the modernization of state authorities, by the beginning of the new century. In the current period, its results have risen to a level that can be a model for any country in the world. This situation is evident in the growth of its economic potential.

The modernization of state authorities in the USA began after Great Britain - in 1993. Reforms in this area were initiated by President Bill Clinton, and Vice President Albert Gore was tasked with coordinating this process. He put forward the following slogan for reforms in this field: "creating a well-functioning and affordable government." In September 1998, the Brookings Institution's Center for Public Management released a report, "Government Reform: A Five-Year Report," prepared by Professor Donald F. Kettle of the University of Pennsylvania, which analyzed the Clinton administration's reform report.

It was noted in the report that the changes implemented are extremely serious, and the difficulties and problems that have arisen in this area require the reforms to take a long time. However, despite this, the modernization of the management sphere of state authorities in the country had shown many achievements. Work in this area is planned to be carried out in three stages, the first stage of which is called "Better performance, less spending".

The reforms initially began with the reduction of civil servants. Although 252,000 employees were planned to be cut at the federal level, 273,000 employees were actually cut.

The government has tasked all federal agencies with adapting to the needs of citizens and thinking less about their own interests. Most government officials have greatly increased the types of services provided to citizens, and for this purpose have switched to cooperation with private firms. The main idea of the reform strategy was aimed at strengthening relations between the government and the people, making political programs popular and understandable.

The reformers put forward the argument that citizens and taxpayers are not clients, and declared that the relationship between the state and the population cannot be likened to the relationship between a seller and a client, on the contrary, this relationship should be similar to the relationship with the shareholders of a large company and its general manager. did The reformers published the following arguments: "citizens, as consumers of public services, want high-quality service and want this service to be affordable: if it snows on the street, they want to clear the street of snow, if there are bumps in the road, they want to re-inflate the tires of their car wheels. wants to pave this road in order not to put it out of business. Residents hope for clean and safe parks, schools with good teachers, police officers who catch criminals quickly, and strict control over the quality of food products. Generally speaking, they want a government that takes responsibility. However, citizens themselves also provide services, that is, they should participate in these reforms. Let's say, an ordinary pharmacist - developing medical programs the outgoing leader is a taxpayer, as is the manager. The family doctor is the first "provider" in the list of all providers. In general, citizens should not play the last role in these reforms. In addition, citizens do not want to pay more taxes for services rendered as taxpayers. Citizens expect great responsibility   from the government."

The concept of reforms has put forward the following comprehensive approaches to this process in order to clarify

the central concept of administrative reforms - "Government Clients":

I.   Citizens as service consumers.
II. Citizens are partners in service delivery.
III. Citizens as supervisors of the state.
IV. Citizens as taxpayers.

A special program of total quality management (TQM) was developed in the country, based on a simple idea: know what citizens need and find a way to provide it. One approach to this process is that civil servants working with the public in the internal client model should tell the government whose interests they represent. This means that managers need to improve contract performance with the help of contract makers. In this way, each manager represents the interests of his group.

Since 1996, the Presidential Administration has begun to transfer a number of ministries to work as "service administration". After 1998, Congress approved the establishment of the first institution of this model. The Department of Education has become a management based on "service blind sales".

The second stage of reforms began in 1994, during which "Reconsider what you are doing!" slogan was put forward.

According to it, significant powers of the state government (including expansion of privatization, trade income and revenues) were transferred to local governments. Main focus focused on discussions on the topic "How can things get out of hand?"

During this period, significant attention was paid to improving the qualifications of the highest categories of state leadership. Also, during this period, businessmen made up the majority of politicians, and they used the privileges of their positions.

In order to prevent corruption in various sectors, a federal high-risk program was developed, which included, first of all, monitoring the state inventory of medicine, control over medical and aviation services, strengthening customs control, control over the loan program for farmers, environment such as improved protection was included.

During this period, the federal government was recognized to be suffering from three major deficits: budget deficits; lack of public trust in the government; lack of people's ideas about administrative reforms.

The third stage of administrative reforms began in 1998. The slogan "America is at the forefront in everything" was put forward. During this period, the following new directions of reforms were defined:

- to transform the agencies that are most demanded by the citizens into fast and efficient administrative structures that can quickly adapt to the needs of the population;
- development of "preventive" management aimed at eliminating administrative problems;
- to give civil servants the right to act more freely, in addition to

the performance of their work, in connection with the increased responsibility for its results;
- development of information provision and service provision.
During this period, the following slogans were announced: "Building a safe and healthy America", "A strong economy" and "The strongest government in management".

During this period, the government paid more attention to the use of horizontal organizational structures. From them, a geographical approach was chosen as a prospective approach. The state administration was traditionally organized by sectors (agriculture, healthcare, trade, defense, etc.).

The conclusions of the experts that the determination of state resources based on the specific needs of the local population will be improved in the organization of management by geographical regions led to the emergence of this new approach of the government. Therefore, based on this new model, relations of administrative management with institutions were built on the basis of horizontal rather than vertical relations.

Another innovation in the US public administration system is the adoption of a government performance measurement program. This program was not only a way to measure the results of the government's activities, but also a means of mutual relations between the state organizations, determining important future activities and finding a solution to the problems that have arisen. The program began to gain importance in improving managers' skills.

Thanks to the program, it became possible to measure effective services and evaluate the services provided in general care. This program was especially important in determining the results of the services provided and the reimbursement of the funds spent on them. The program has created many opportunities for the development of federal government management. As a result of measuring the government's performance, the citizens have an idea of what they are getting in return for the taxes they pay.

Also, the government had the opportunity to determine how effective its activities are and to correct the mistakes and shortcomings it has made.

By this time, it was a new important principle of state administration sips were formed:

- formation of effective structures instead of official state management structures;
- strengthen competition, not monopoly;
- the main focus is not on bureaucratic structures focus on customer needs;
- not to the extent of citizens' consumption, but to those who receive it pay attention to their income;
- decentralization of state authorities.

Osborn and Gebler, theorists of reform in the USA, in their book "Government Reform" developed a new direction of government activity - "a simple and clear way of a new approach to work with social business." According to him, while earlier centralization and a large number of standard regulations, the lack of ability of public administration organizations to adapt quickly, tendencies to increase the number of public service employees were prioritized, now the reforms to eliminate them continued. The government focused on eliminating complacency and complacency in the bureaucracy, and developing initiative and efficiency in them. In this process, quality, efficiency and the use of management technologies in business appeared as the main principles.

During the study of the results of administrative reforms over the past five years, it was shown that the process of finding solutions to problems in this area will continue for a long time. Because, on the one hand, there were positive changes in the reforms, but on the other hand, negative situations began to show themselves. For example, one-sixth of all civil servants were cut, while the Department of Justice (as a result of the hiring of auditors and inspectors for newly created services) saw a 22 percent increase. But, nevertheless, the reduction of the bureaucracy, the expansion of the control system led to an increase in the responsibility of the state administration to citizens.

The results of the reforms showed that the reform of the government ended the budget deficit, and the people's trust in the government began to increase. However, at the same time, the population's interest in administrative reforms did not develop much. The expansion of management in the administration caused the emergence of ideas of radical change of state authorities. Making new changes every year in the US administration has become a common practice.

Important reforms in the modernization of US government organizations continued under President George W. Bush in a new form. He initiated the establishment of electronic government (Electronic Government, e-Government). As a result of reforms in this area, 20 thousand government websites (consisting of 30 million web pages) were opened. If 86% of the US population uses the Internet, 60% of them start using government information and other information related to various public surveillance services.

In 2003, President Bush created the position of chief executive in the federal government, giving them the status of first deputy secretary in each department. Their main task was to connect the results of the work with the budget indicators, improve the quality of personnel, improve financial discipline, and develop modern management factors such as the introduction of information technologies.

Of course, this new position began to improve adaptation to the requirements of the market economy. Also, the changes at this time were reflected in the introduction of corporate management principles into the public service structures. A special Management Council was formed under the President, which included general managers of important ministries and institutions, several assistants of the President, and the deputy head of the vice president's office. The main task of the council was defined as assisting the President in reforming the government in terms of the vertical hierarchy of power.

After Barack Obama came to power in the USA in 2009 amid the global financial and economic crisis, the concept of reforming the financial compliance system was developed at his initiative. Important attention was paid to preventing the re-emergence of systemic crises in the US economy. The US Federal Reserve has been empowered to manage systemic risks. A consumer protection agency was established to protect real estate debtors, credit card holders, and customers using various financial services.

The state of the United States as a result of the modernization of the administration of public authorities in the world shows that it has advanced in the field of administrative reforms.

Although the people's trust in the government is not very high in the country, it still ranks high in terms of quality indicators of public administration. The results of the research conducted by the World Bank (The Worldwide Governance Indicators (WGI) project) aimed at studying the quality and effectiveness of state governance announced the index of the effectiveness of government and civil service activities in serving the population based on the growth rates in 1996-2014. These studies evaluate the quality and efficiency of public administration. In it, the provision of state services and the levels of its improvement are determined on the basis of inter-state and comparative analyses. According to this index, the USA obtained 89.9-92 points in the 100-point system in 1996-2014 and is the leading country in the world in this field.

According to the study, the trust of the US population is not in the public service, but in the official in the public administration. In general, it was found that the population of the USA is a leading country with a high level of trust in the state authorities.

Also, at the present time, indexes of the level of transparency of relations in the economy of each state, the functioning of market mechanisms, and the extent to which its public administration is connected with service activities are being developed. According to the research conducted by the Price water house Cooper company, "The lack of transparency in some countries", the USA can be shown as an example in this field.

Research shows that as a result of the development of management technologies, the level of corruption in the USA has decreased, anti-corruption control processes have increased, and modern methods of its detection have been developed. The USA has also taken the first place in the development of electronic legal texts. According to the United Nations "Research on the topic of e-government", the United States ranks seventh in the world in terms of introducing e-government into the management system. The global average of the E-Government Development Index (EGDI) was 0.4712, while the US index was 0.8748.3

In addition, the USA is a leading country in the supply of electronic resources to other countries. It ranks 6th in the world in terms of electronic services. In the same electronic way, providing services to the population and providing interaction with state authorities plays the main role.

It is clear from the analysis that the US government is the world's leading country in terms of modernization of public authorities, increasing the efficiency and scope of their services to citizens. The experience of the USA in this field is important for the countries that are going through the transition period, and the application of this experience based on the harmony of national traditions is important for them to overcome various crisis situations.

CONTROL QUESTIONS

1. What does the experience of modernization of British public authorities include?
2. What are the fundamental changes in the field of modernization of state power in Great Britain at the beginning of the 21st century?
3. What does the experience of modernization of US government organizations include?

5-THEME: MODERNIZATION EXPERIENCE OF STATE POWER SYSTEM IN ROMANO-GERMANIC COUNTRIES

Plan:

1. Modernization of state power in France.
2. The process of modernization of the state power system in Germany.
3. Modernization of public authorities in Germany institutional reforms.

Until the 20th century, France, as a strongly centralized power, paid significant attention to the vertical interaction of state administration organizations. But the strong economic and social development in European and North American countries began to put the need for development in front of the French state. Of course, the slowing down of economic development in the country, the beginning of signs of socio-economic instability were inextricably linked with the activity of the state administration system. That is why the French government started reforms to modernize public authorities from the beginning of the 80s of the 20th century.

In these reforms, significant attention was paid to changes in the transfer of powers of central and higher state organizations to lower organizations and self-governing organizations, which is mainly called decentralization.

During this period, complex administrative-territorial structures functioned in France, they were traditional forms: commune - canton - operated according to the district-department-region hierarchical scheme. Among them, the canton and district were far from the status of a general administrative body, and they were considered the territory of some special administrative organizations. On March 2, 1982, the law "On the rights and freedoms of the communes, departments and regions" was announced, according to which the region acquired the status of a territorial community, and the entire territory of France was divided into regions. According to this law, aspects of control over local self-government organizations have been drastically changed: the rights of control over local executive power have been removed from local government representatives, and they can form representative organizations of their own choosing. Certain changes were also made to the status of communes, which also applied to large central cities (such as Paris, Lyon, Marseille). The island of Corsica was given a special status due to its ethnic differences.

In 1983, a special law was adopted on the harmonization of relations between state organizations and self-governing organizations, and the powers of self-governing organizations were expanded: they were given the right to dispose of material resources and financial resources. The territory of France was divided into 27 regions, each of which was recognized as self-governing territorial communities. Regions gained responsibility for ensuring socio-economic, cultural and scientific development in their territories, and each of them also got the right to preserve its identity. Regions have their own budget and have the right to adopt their own socio-economic development plans. It was stipulated that the legal acts adopted by them should not conflict with the government's decisions and that the territorial unity of the country should be preserved.

After that, there are issues of coordination of relations of regions with departments and communes clarified. The decentralization law of 1983 included the principle that communes, departments, and regions were given the right to self-governance, without any of them being patronized by others.

Some issues, for example, financial and grant giving, were decided at the regional level, and although the commune and the department were on its territory, the independent self-government of the commune and department was established by law. Rules for the operation of representative organizations in regions, departments and communes were established. The executive power was headed by the chairman of the regional council. Of course, these reforms also created the need to modernize the central state authorities.

From the second half of the 80s of the 20th century, the administrative reforms in France mainly focused on the development of management and the creation of the French model of the information state. The government's strategy in this area focused on increasing the types of public services for the population, bringing the government closer to the population, and seriously democratizing the administration. During this period, the population trusted civil society more than the government, businessmen, and the media. Since it is difficult for the government to win the trust of the population on its own, the cooperation of politics, business and civil society was given importance during this period. It was hoped that this tripartite cooperation would be strong at any level - global, regional and local.

Reforms in France can be conventionally divided into two major stages: social- democratic and Gaullist reforms (F. Mitterrand, J. Chirac); Conservative reforms (N. Sarkozy).

At the first stage of the reforms, the slogan of the reforms was announced in a social-democratic spirit: "Let the administration be at the service of the citizens!" However, there was no talk of bringing the principles of the market economy into public administration, but the main priority was focused on increasing the democratic aspects of public administration and public service. During this period, market mechanisms were not introduced into the activities of justice and public order maintenance organizations.

General leadership of the reforms was carried out by the state administration and the Ministry of State Reforms. By the end of 1990, two more institutions were established to coordinate reforms: the Inter- ministerial Committee on State Reforms and the Inter-ministerial Directorate on State Reforms. The committee meets several times a year with the participation of all ministers, and it takes the main responsibility for reforms.

The board was responsible for preparing for decision-making and implementing them. The government tasked all state agencies and institutions with the task of developing long-term modernization plans for each institution. In order to financially support the reforms, the ministries, regional and departmental services have established a fund for state reforms.

In 1997, the government adopted a program to bring France into the information society. Based on the program, as a result of the use of modern communication technologies, communication and information exchange between services were established, inter-institutional coordination was facilitated, and speedy execution of decisions began to be ensured. The availability of public services for consumers - private individuals and enterprises was announced through the websites of the ministries. List of services, contact addresses, etc. on the sites information was published regularly. It has become customary for the main decisions of the government, laws, and decrees to be published in the official notice - "Journal officiel".

An inter-ministerial service of technical support for the development of information and communication technologies was established to implement the reforms. With the help of this service, in 2000, the official website of the state administration was opened on the Internet, providing access to 2,600 national and local, 2,000 European and national government websites.

According to the law adopted in 1983, the French government began to introduce the principles of decentralization into the system of public authorities. According to the well-known French political scientist Guy Sorman, the abolition of guardianship by the central state authorities led to the strengthening of local and regional authorities from economic and political aspects. 3

New methods of management that effectively use information technologies have begun to combine the advantages of decentralization with the speed of information networks and ensure the transparent progress of reforms.

From the year 2000, the results of decentralization began to be seen: the qualifications of civil servants increased, their inclination to initiative increased, the employees of self- government organizations became professional, and their qualities of efficiency were formed. Local state organizations began to operate freely in organizational issues and personnel allocation.

Central institutions were limited only to the powers of developing national activities and strategic tasks.

Ministers were also given great powers. He got the right to reorganize ministries independently. They are basically strategic tasks - planning, forecasting, control was busy with the activities of making, and gave the previous powers to the local authorities.

On July 12, 1996, a special inter-ministerial decree established the "General form of service contracts for Aho League". In these three-year general contracts, it was determined to list the services of public servants to be sold blindly to consumers, the means of their implementation, and the indicators of obligations to be sold. Such contractual relations began to give greater independence to decentralized organizations and organizations.

Administrative reforms in France have brought management and state organizations closer to each other in the business sector, improved the quality of services to the population, and accelerated the execution of contractual obligations. According to the Law "On

Standardization of Public Service" adopted on April 12, 2000, all state organizations and organizations are required to fulfill certain obligations based on the quality of their services to citizens. In particular, it was made mandatory for civil servants to issue a receipt for every appeal they received from the government, indicating the person's name and address. On the day of receipt of the application, a rule was introduced that the deadline for responding to the application should be considered from the date indicated on the postmark or from the date of sending the e-mail.

According to this new law, the procedures for receiving citizens by civil servants have been simplified. The population has more opportunities to familiarize themselves with administrative documents. Procedures for making payments to residents have also been eased. Communal services, local organizations were provided with payment terminals, payment of payments by bank cards became freer, issuance of technical passport for cars, obtaining driver's license, the processes of issuing citizenship documents, issuing visas, and making customs payments have been cleared of bureaucratic obstacles.

Administrative formalities in the registration of enterprises have been completed. The Secretariat for Small and Medium- sized Enterprises has been engaged in this field. The terms of issuing certificates to business representatives, registration of enterprises and firms have been shortened, and the declaration of the payment of value added tax has also been simplified.

During this period, the directive decision of the government to adopt the annual plan of each ministry to simplify the administrative formalities in its field gained importance in this field. In order to harmonize this area, a special commission on simplification of administrative procedures was established, and it was assigned the task of summarizing the information provided by all ministries, and then handing them over to the inter-ministerial department for state reforms.

At the request of the government, a number of measures were taken to improve the quality of services provided to the population by the public service: publication of information for the public, holding an open day, distribution of advertising materials in the areas where the public service is performed, encouraging public service employees based on letters of thanks from the public on Internet sites, and etc

Another innovation in this area was to bring the public service closer to the customers. Special public service centers were opened to provide comprehensive and efficient service; they were provided with special statuses, and their work procedures and duties were determined. These centers provided the provision of services of various state institutions in one place. In one center, government agencies, social organizations, local self- government organizations, and private firms and firms that fulfill state orders served the population at the same time.

In the centers, employees began to provide advice to residents, assist them in writing their demands and transfer them to higher authorities, and study the opinions of residents regarding the provided services. In 2000, 300 centers operated.

As another way to get closer to the population, administrative and legal assistance centers were established. Such centers were opened in residential areas on the outskirts of the city, in "problem" areas where the unemployed and people in need of social protection made up the majority. In these centers, adaptation of citizens' appeals in cases where violations of the law do not pose a great danger is to be adapted. In this place, lawyers provide free advice to residents, representatives of victims' aid associations are on duty day and night, and the Red Cross organization and its employees are accepted.

In the reforms of the modernization of public authorities in France, important attention was paid to the training of civil service personnel in accordance with the new era. In 2000, the monitoring committee on employment in the civil service was established in order to improve the quality and qualification of civil service personnel, and to promote the development of work efficiency. In addition to conducting statistical research in this field, he began to work in such directions as participation in the formation of an information collection system, employment forecasting, and issemination of information in this field. In addition, each ministry was assigned the tasks of future management of personnel, employment and planning of needs of specialists. At the same time, measures were taken to remove restrictions on the transfer of an employee from one enterprise to another, ignoring his wishes and obstacles to meeting other professional needs. The legal grounds for taking into account the results of the personnel's work have been created in the consistent promotion of the staff to higher positions.

Also, a system of continuous professional development of civil servants was developed. The National Center of Distance Education regularly develops new technologies of professional training by means of television and information technologies. Conditions were also created for civil servants to receive new generation literature and educational programs on Internet sites.

At the beginning of the 21st century in France, a total of 2.6 million officials of various levels made up 12% of the total employed population. 230,000 of them are included in the category of civil servants, even if they do not belong to the official category. 1.1 percent of employees work at the local municipal level, 900,000 of them at the commune (community) level, 160,000 in departments, and 24,000 in districts. However, in the next 6-7 years, the number of civil servants decreased significantly.

In the 2007 elections in France, the right-wing conservative party led by Nicolas Sarkozy came to power instead of the Social Democrats. In 2008-2009, a new period of modernization of state authorities began. President Sarkozy set a new record in this field by promoting 490 reform initiatives. France had not undergone such large-scale reforms since the de Gaulle era. The reforms were carried out in five main areas: constitutional, financial, immigration, law enforcement and combating unemployment. Amendments were made to 47 of the 89 articles of the Constitution adopted in 1958. The idea of "modernization of the institutions of the Fifth Republic" was put forward as the slogan of the reforms. During this period, the Presidential Institute was also reformed:

- limitation of running for the presidency (no one can run for office more than twice in a row);
- based on the importance of the nation's socio-economic life, protection of human rights and freedoms, the candidate for the highest state position is heard by the standing commissions of the National Assembly and the Senate. If three-fifths of those participating in the meeting vote against his candidacy, then the parliament can veto the candidate;
- the "full seizure of power" by the president must be carried out

under the supervision of the Constitutional Council in accordance with Article 16 of the Constitution (in emergency situations);
- the president no longer heads the Supreme Council of Magistracy (the highest body of the French judicial community), but he appoints an ombudsman - a human rights defender;
- finally, the president is a joint member of both chambers of the parliament can "take the floor" at the meeting (like the US model).
In this way, the priorities of reforms of the modernization of public authorities in France were to make the activities of public officials more effective and qualitative, to strengthen the democratic foundations of public administration, and to make public services close to the population and operate with effective results. These reforms took on a collective character and focused on the formation of an information state in France. This situation was important for the country not to suffer much from the complications of the world financial and economic crisis, and for further increasing the state's potential.

As in all European countries, in Germany, the modernization of state authorities on the basis of the requirements of the current era began in the 90s of the 20th century. During this period, the ideas of New Social Management (SIM) in Europe began to spread widely. But Germany was still at an average level in the field of implementation of the new social management. During this period, budget expenditures at all levels of state administration increased, the process of reunification of

Germany required large amounts of money. Also, during this period, the fact that the main ideas of GDP were aimed at reducing costs and increasing the efficiency of management made political circles very interested.

In discussions at the highest levels, the turn towards the modernization of state authorities took place at the initiative of KGST (Communale Gemeinschaftstelle für Verwaltungsmanagement - Municipal Association of Administrative Management). In 1991, the KGST took a sharp turn: joining the debate on GDP and promoting the "New Management Model" (Neues Steuerungsmodell) as the German model of GDP, based on the modernization concept developed in Tilburg, the Netherlands.

Important components of GDP modernization consists of: KGST's "New Model of Management" (NYAM) was aimed at eliminating the features of the traditional model of general management through decentralization. The middle and lower responsible links of the management get the right to independently make decisions on the use and movement of important types of resources (funds, personnel, organizational structure) without receiving orders from above.

Accordingly, the municipal association of administrative management - KGST undertakes internal control instead of hierarchical subordination of lower levels of management. In doing so, legal standards are strictly enforced various indicators are widely used in execution, as well as information technologies and schemes in this process. In this, the main attention is focused on the realization of management "costs and achievements - final results".

1. New social management - the necessary elements of the new model of management are introduced instead of the directions of social administration: from the "input dimensions" in the work activity (legal norms and allocated budget resources) as a result of the activity, they become the final performance results (clarification of goals, especially budget saving management). performed by the riyat). This means that social administration "economies" are achieved not only by following legal norms, but also as a result of increasing the efficiency of spent funds.

2. Municipal association of administrative management - KGST model is more related to political management compared to the New Social Model (YAIM), which envisages the increase and expansion of the control powers of the elected advisory board over the local administration (especially the dimensions that change in the budget processes). Unlike the traditional budget, that is, instead of trying to strictly implement the volume of available funds and the income and expenditure parts of a separate budget, the budget is focused on getting the final results, and it represents the total financial sum.

In the new model of governance, the political attention of the elected budget councils is focused on making major decisions (instead of solving the previously obvious and less important issues) within the framework of local policy-making.

In accordance with the growing influence of KGST, the "New Model of General Management" spread rapidly among self- governing organizations. "New Model of Management" in ten years, almost all (92%) of German local administrations with a population of at least 10,000 modernized their management system in 1990-2000, while 80% of this was done only on the basis of the KGST model.

Local communities (the lowest self-governing organizations) was given the following powers:

1) private - the team hires personnel on its own initiative selection, promotion and dismissal;
2) financial - collected income and expenses right of disposal;
3) organizational - authority to adjust its internal structure based on local conditions;
4) making decisions in the legal-communal sphere, implementing useful constructions in one's territory;
5) tax - raising or lowering community fees, collecting various contributions, collecting internal taxes and other revenues from citizens in their territory.

In Germany, in addition to regional communities at the federal and state levels, there is also the concept of "community" (like a neighborhood), which, while consisting of small communities, has the same status as large cities. Communities have been defined as the status of cities that do not have district importance.

The reforms of the late 20th and early 21st centuries continued at the same time as the processes of unification of East and West Germany. The process of modernization of state administration organizations in East Germany was aimed at drastic changes.

Nevertheless, in 1990, the reform of administrative-territorial and local self-government organizations was completed. Reforms as a result, instead of the previous 189 districts, 87 districts were established; At the municipal (local self-government) level, the number of administrative units and staff has been greatly reduced, and new standards of representation in councils have been established.

Brandenburg, Saxony, Thuringia, Upper Pomerania adopted new regional laws on local self-government organizations - municipal constitutions.

As a result, the differences in the local administration of western and eastern Germany were abolished.

Administrative reforms in Germany were aimed at introducing less bureaucratic and less expensive forms of governance in cities and communities. Provision of guaranteed services instead of expensive public service prices, an effort was made to create competitiveness between them.

In large cities of Germany, such as Berlin, Munich, Cologne, Hamburg, where millions of people live, civil counseling centers aimed at facilitating citizens' relations with the administration were established. Employees of civil counseling offices help to find the necessary organization, distribute various information among the population. Most of the counseling centers conduct dialogues between residents and the city administration in the form of "direct telephone communication".

The motto of the telephone service is "We help!" We will find the address you want! We will search!' was formed by sponsoring invitations such as This situation made life of citizens much easier.

The new management model in Germany differs sharply from the Anglo-Saxon model, which is business to municipal management was based on the gradual assimilation of management in the field. The motto of "New Public Management" was based on the democratic values that "the state bureaucracy should be reduced, and citizens' participation in decision-making and social work should be increased." The German management strategy was based on the wide participation of various regional associations and networks of various structures in the process of self-management, and regular monitoring of work results. These circumstances ensured the gradualness of the reforms and their development on the basis of mutual consensus.

The municipal association of administrative management - KGST put forward the following slogan: "From bureaucratic coordination to service-based organization of work through a new management model." The new management model focused primarily on improving the quality of local government services.

The main idea was to decentralize administrative structures, increase their accountability to customers, and organize monitoring of the quality of service sales.

At the same time, the working style of the local administration has changed radically, its main focus has been on ensuring consumer rights.

By 2000, the scale of reforms had spread to 90 percent of the country's cities. In order to help spread new models and experiences, the Bertelsmann and

Hans-Böckler Foundations have established the German Cities of Tomorrow association.

Another direction of modernization of state authorities in Germany is institutional reforms aimed at further development of democratic values in the country. For this purpose, the law on direct election of mayors was adopted. According to it, the influence of political parties on the support of candidates was reduced, and the rights of voters in this area were expanded.

At the same time, the institution of a local referendum is established, and it can be held at the initiative of 10-15 percent of the population. It is expressed in regulatory documents. Residents became more active in local decision-making. Local government organizations were forced to take into account the interests of the population, and all democratic procedures were formed.

A movement of new civil initiatives was formed. They began to raise issues of environmental protection, kindergartens and children's playgrounds, transportation, schools, and urban infrastructure.

Community and city councils, although they do not have the right to pass laws, have begun to perform parliamentary tasks to some extent: clarifying and adopting the budget; making decisions related to the city and its management; adoption of local legislative acts; determining the amount of funds to be paid for waste transportation. The elected representatives of the people began to express the previous state communal policy in their activities based on the new legislation.

Community councils began to provide social support to the elderly who did not have the right to receive assistance or allowances for their illness. Annual expenditures of municipal councils in the social sphere made 40 billion euros on average across the country. Almost 2 million people a year have the right to regularly receive financial assistance.

Regional management organizations began to operate on the basis of the following division of powers in managing all social spheres: execution of the tasks set from above and the independent management process of local management organizations. According to the law, self-governing organizations must obey orders of federal and regional (territorial) organizations. However, most of the social issues in the territory of the community are performed as a result of independent activities of the self-governing organizations. For example, they independently build sports facilities and swimming pools, pedestrian walkways construction, beautification of recreation parks, beautification of the territory, formation of local transport network and their use. Therefore, they began to repair, decorate and beautify cultural buildings in their regions independently.

The financial basis of communities began to be formed on the basis of utility payments, craft taxes, street lighting and sewerage fees, fees from vacant buildings, small community taxes, income from fishing and recreation.

Privatization has been an important area of reform in the utility sector in Germany. For example, the city of Essen owns more than 50 percent of the profits (shares) of 37 of them in partnership with 50 joint-stock companies.

These enterprises include local fair, labor and employment society. Joint-stock companies are managed in a private capitalistic way. 2 In the current period, the city market began to buy various buildings, schools, waste processing machines, various office buildings, and private enterprises at low prices.

All self-governing organizations have become multifunctional, and their number has reached the following amount by the present time: 12,600 municipalities (cities and communities); 320 counties. In addition to their activities based on the interests of their territory and residents, they also work on the basis of powers delegated by higher management organizations.

Local authorities ensure the implementation of 80% of all legislative decisions adopted by the federal government, national and European Union parliaments. Also local authorities organizations spend almost 75% of social investments.

In the administrative service at the level of local government, 30 percent of all employees in the social sector of the state perform administrative activities.

Since the 90s of the 20th century, the civil service system has also been modernized in Germany. In fact, the reforms in this area are based on the civil service laws passed in 1957-1985. As a result of the modernization of this sector, the following features of the public service model were formed:

1) the role of politically appointed or elected officials is strong in the public service system, especially in the area of strategic management decision-making;
2) at each level of management, the civil service system is clearly organized on the basis of the powers established on the basis of regulatory documents (up to the division of the powers of decision-making and their

execution) and the established principles of career subordination;

3) the presence of a complex and multi-level system of selection from among the graduates of higher educational institutions for public service;

4) the fact that the civil servant has a high social status, the existence of mechanisms for achieving prestige and standards of professional ethics, the introduction of the institute of honorary official;

5) the creation of a system of guarantees of protection of civil servants from legal and social aspects, the existence of the principle of "lifetime appointment";

6) the fact that upward growth in positions, wages and benefits depend on seniority and position level;

7) prioritization of specialists who have received legal education in public service.

It is clear from the analysis that the work of modernization of the state authorities in Germany based on the requirements of the current era began in the 90s of the 20th century and continues until now. These reforms further improved the rule of law in the country, created conditions for civil society institutions to operate based on the interests of the population. The results of this modernization were also important in increasing Germany's economic power.

CONTROL QUESTIONS

1. What does the modernization of state power in France include?
2. What does the process of modernization of the system of state power in Germany involve?
3. What do institutional reforms include in the modernization of state authorities in Germany?

6-THEME MODERNIZATION OF THE PUBLIC SERVICE PROVISION AND MANAGEMENT SYSTEM: CHINESE AND JAPANESE MODEL

Plan:

1. *The Chinese model of modernization of the state management system.*
2. *Characteristics of administrative reforms in China.*
3. *Fundamental reforms to update the Japanese public administration system.*

One of the characteristics of modernized societies is the development of civil society and the legal state or their elements. The results of China's modernization can be cited as an objection to this idea. However, China cannot be said to have achieved progress through reforms unrelated to Western modernization.

In China, the factors of modernization in the West were also effectively used. Initially, Deng Xiaoping, the architect of China's modernization, put forward 4 principles to preserve the socialist system: not to deviate from the path of socialism; dictatorship of the proletariat; the party, as well as the leadership role of Marxism-Leninism and Mao Zedong's ideas.1 These principles increased the tendency of the Chinese leadership and political elite to support reforms. After that, Deng Xiaoping developed a new economic policy ("Building socialism based on China's characteristics"). Its principles were as follows:

- to create conditions for people to get rich through their honest work, both in the village and in the city;
- allowing certain components of capitalism to exist as a supplement to the development of socialist productive forces;
- fight liberalism firmly to prevent the population from being polarized by wealth and income levels.

The reforms started in 1979 supported the contractor farmer, craftsman, and businessman, and hundreds of thousands of enterprises were established in districts, villages, and small towns. The system of distribution relations was changed, it was transferred to the system of tax Opportunities were created for a number of enterprises to purchase new equipment and technologies at the expense of their income. By 1985, taxes accounted for half of corporate income, and the other half remained at the disposal of enterprises. Some enterprises were allowed to conduct economic activities in cooperation with foreign enterprises. Steel, copper, cement were distributed by the state, and the experience of centralized distribution of all other resources was abandoned. State properties were also put into execution. Trade, catering, medical practice, tailoring, car and bicycle repair were taken over by the private sector. Special economic zones and new technology zones have mushroomed.

The economy was rebuilt on the basis of pluralism. In order to attract foreign investments in China, 20,000 projects were approved in 1998, contracts with foreign capital worth 52.2 billion dollars were signed. In 2005, foreign investments amounted to 120 billion dollars.

This year, the positive trade balance amounted to 101.9 billion dollars. As a result, China's GDP in 2002–2007 (GDP) increased by an average of 10.6 percent per year and reached 65.5 percent. The economy of the People's Republic of China has far surpassed all the "Asian Tigers". China's GDP grew by 6.9% in 2015, and by 6.6% in 2016.1 A wealthy class of small owners has formed in the country.

It is clear from the analysis that the Chinese economy also gave its positive results as a result of applying the laws of the modern market economy formed in the West. The state authorities have adopted methods and mechanisms based on the requirements of market economy relations into their management system (as was the case with the NEP in the 20s of the 20th century and during the reconstruction of the second half of the 80s). Universal human values of having economic rights and freedoms and protecting them were included in the socialist ideology.

The Chinese Communist Party has also been reformed to the extent that it can adapt to the demands of the market economy. In the second half of the 80s in China, the difference from the reconstruction in the former union is that the Chinese Communist Party adapted to the principles and laws of the market economy at the level of state policy. In the former union, the head of state pursued a policy against the leaders of the regional party organizations, which represent the real power in the regions, thereby depriving them of the real power and resources that would support the reforms.

In general, as a conclusion, it can be said that society can be modernized even in the conditions of different ideologies or state systems. For this, first of all, it is necessary to apply the laws of the market economy in practice, to form a class of owners, to adapt the state and legislation to the development of private property, and to fully support the spirit and desire of individual wealth acquisition.

Modernization of society and state is evident from the economic background of most developed countries, as well as China. In order to implement the reforms, first of all, it is necessary to modernize the system of state administration organizations. Because, in the countries that are going through the transition period, the problems of employment of the population, ideological confusion, the presence of layers of the population in need of social protection, threats and factors such as the attack of various foreign ideas place a great responsibility on the state authorities in the modernization of the society. That is why, in most countries, the state authorities are first modernized, and then the conditions for the modernization of the entire society are created.

In the last quarter of the 20th century, a new "Chinese model" of modernization of state power and administration was formed. Although the influence of Marxism was strong in China during this period, the ideas of liberalism began to enter this country from the 90s of the 20th century, and it began to be clearly visible in social, especially economic life. At the end of the 70s of the 20th century, due to the economic changes and transparency policy carried out under the leadership of Deng Xiaoping, the "father" of Chinese reforms, doctrines contrary to the tenets of Marxism, including liberal ideas and views, began to enter the state administration and economy. Despite the initial resistance and repression of liberal opposition, they soon had a strong influence on the worldview of the intelligentsia of the general public. It is noteworthy that the Chinese leadership has taken the path of using the doctrine of liberalism as an ideological theoretical factor that motivates the further acceleration of economic reforms.

Thus, in the socialist country - China, liberalism was officially recognized as a system of political views and a theory of modernization of public administration. This situation began to mean that the Chinese leadership is striving towards the fundamental reform of the country's economy, the establishment of a "Chinese" legal state based on the power of law, and a civil society.

At present, it is the leader in the world in terms of economic growth, it provides material support to more than 1 billion 300 million people.

It has become customary for the western world to call this country, which supplies the world market with various products, a land of strange secrets, unique ancient traditions, and people with a special mentality. Of course, the fundamental changes in China have their own reasons. For example, China's transition to a market economy is very different from its Western models, just as earlier Chinese socialism was never purely communist. In this sense, it was not for nothing that many people were surprised that the leadership of the Chinese state became a supporter of liberal ideas and views, democratic values. In fact, it was an amazing fact that he combined the doctrine of liberalism, which protects the interests of human freedom and rights, with communist beliefs.

However, by objectively approaching the reality of Chinese society, it is possible to observe rapid development, progress and renewal in all spheres of the country's life. In fact, over the past 20 years, this country has made incomparable progress in terms of socio-economic development, the formation of modern market infrastructures, and the improvement of the population's standard of living and material well-being.

It has reached the level of developed countries in terms of some economic indicators, and has taken the first place in the world in terms of economic growth rates. That is why many scientists and ink sellers began to predict that the 21st century will be the century of China.

The essence of the "Chinese miracle" and the main reasons for its successful future are the fact that the unique mentality and national characteristics of the Chinese people were taken into account when choosing a new path of development, as well as the "three steps" development proposed by the "architect of reforms" Deng Xiaoping in the early 80s of the last century. is explained by the adoption of the strategy and its consistent and steady implementation.

If in the 50s of the last century in China, slogans such as "we will reach England in 15 years" were economically baseless, contrary to the real reality, the "three step" strategy is a completely new approach, including gradual implementation of reforms, based on the principles of maintaining the leading role of the state, socially protecting disadvantaged groups of the population, and creating the necessary conditions for attracting foreign investment. The theoretical basis of this policy is expressed in this concept. What was the essence of this new concept?

The concept of "three steps" envisaged the fundamental reform of the country's economy and, ultimately, raising it to the level of the most developed countries, improving the material well-being and standard of living of the people. This concept was far from the existing reality, devoid of any imaginary goals or objectives. Incidentally, Deng Xiaoping himself was famous for his ability to approach reality pragmatically. In the early 1970s, when journalists asked him how compatible the concept of reform was with the ideals of the socialist system, Deng Xiaoping replied, "Will the cat be white or black?" - what difference does it make, after all, he can catch a mouse! he answered. Therefore, the concept of "Three Steps" was not based on some abstract ideological beliefs, but on clear economic analysis and thinking.

According to it, the main economic indicator is to increase the country's gross domestic product (GDP) twice in the first stage (1982-1989), four times in the second stage (1990-1999), and in the third stage (up to 2050)) GDP per capita was planned to reach four thousand dollars. The tasks of the first two stages were completed ahead of schedule. The third phase is also in full swing.

Currently, China is among the leading countries in terms of gross domestic product and attracting foreign investment is standing. So, since the end of the 70s of the last century, the reforms of liberalizing all spheres of social life and the policy of openness, which have been consistently implemented in China, created the ground for the integration of liberalism and socialist ideas in this country. However, debates continue about the essence of modern Chinese liberalism, its main ideas and principles. For example, although intellectuals and ordinary citizens support liberal democratic values, the ideas of freedom and liberty, it can be observed that most of the officials claim that they are "cleansed" of liberal ideas and support some kind of abstract democratic system. However, in practice, it is observed that the Chinese leadership is looking for measures to liberalize all areas of the country's life, especially the economy, and is making great progress in this area.

In the early stages of China's reform and opening-up policy, Deng Xiaoping began to create a national concept of a market economy. Its essence is that the liberalization of the country's economy, the process of privatization, the emergence of various forms of property, and the influx of foreign investments should not damage the foundations of the current social system. In his speech at the 14th National Congress of the Communist Party of China (1992), Deng Xiaoping spoke about these issues and put forward the following idea: "The main goal of reforming the country's economy is the formation of a socialist market economy system."

Nevertheless, from the very beginning of the reforms, the Chinese leadership faces the problem of liberalizing human rights and freedoms, the authority of economic regions, and the social, political, and spiritual life of the country. In the late 1980s, a new political force appeared in the country - the "For

Democracy" movement events in Beijing on June 4, 1989 showed that different sections of the population, especially the youth and intellectuals, will not back down from the struggle for their political interests. Although these demonstrations were suppressed by the use of force, they did not fail to influence the liberalization of the country's civil society, the further acceleration of reforms, and the modernization of state power and administrative organizations. Solving such complex issues, i.e., the basis of modernization - in the implementation of the policy of liberalization, the main attention was paid to the reform of the economy, especially agriculture.

In the 50s and 60s of the 20th century, when there were agricultural communes, issues such as where to plant what, when and how much to plant, what fertilizers to use, to whom to sell the product, at what price, were decided only from above, and the farmer made any decisions independently. did not have the right to receive. However, by the end of the 70s, as a result of the abolition of centralized management methods, modernization of management organizations and economic reforms, hundreds of thousands of family companies were established instead of communes and centrally managed agricultural enterprises. After that, although the land remained in the state treasury, the management powers of the companies were given to the property owners themselves, that is, the state authorities were decentralized. The owner got the right to run an independent farm. This long-term administrative and economic policy not only fully provided the country's population with agricultural products, but also served to export their surplus and sharply increase the standard of living of the rural population.

By the 80s of the 20th century, special attention was paid to the privatization of state-owned enterprises and opening a wide path to entrepreneurship in China. They were stopped from being managed by state agencies, management functions were given to entrepreneurs and heads of enterprises. This is the case caused the introduction of important amendments to the current legislation and the Constitution, which provide for the protection of private entrepreneurship based on the requirements of the market economy. As a result, hundreds of thousands of small enterprises and firms, millions of private entrepreneurs appeared in the country. Currently, more than 320,000 foreign-invested enterprises are operating in China. Therefore, no matter where you go in the world, there are a lot of products marked "Made in China". Previously, raw materials, food, and light industrial products were more among the exported goods, but now, the weight of modern electronic equipment, advanced technologies, and know-how is increasing year by year. In the current period, China (416 billion US dollars) took the next place after Japan (806 billion US dollars) in terms of foreign exchange reserves. Between 1977 and 1997, China's trade relations with the United States alone increased 40 times and reached 119.5 billion US dollars. In the last decade of the last century, China's economic growth rate reached an average of 10 percent per year, which began to show how much potential and power this country has.

A distinctive feature of the administrative reforms in China is that it is aimed at implementation within the framework of the Chinese Communist Party (CCP), which decided to build a "socialist market economy". If the current administrative reforms were initiated by the decision of the 14th Congress of the Communist Party of China in 1993 and the decision of the Central Committee of the

Communist Party of China in November 1993 "Some Issues of Building a Socialist Market Economy System" as a modernization of the management organizations of state power. In it, it was planned to widely use macroeconomic adjustment of the state as a market tool for the optimal distribution of resources in the country. The goal of administrative reforms is to shift from direct to indirect administrative control and to increase management efficiency with the help of control and macro coordination.

The main modernization of public administration and service directions were as follows:

- reducing the number of the state apparatus;
- Reorganization of the State Council;
- development of a new effective personnel policy through careful selection, training, training and placement of personnel.

Starting from 1996, the 20-year program of transition to a new administrative management system, adapting it to modern market economy relations, began to be implemented. This period was supposed to end in 2015. "Small government in a big society" was defined as the main direction of indirect management, controlling and maintaining balance in the economy. The term of each congress of the KPK represented each stage of this modernization, and the reforms were carried out in four stages.

The first stage (1993-1998) The XIV Congress of the Communist Party of China decided to create a solid legal basis for the formation of a modern market economy. The leadership of the Communist Party of China adopted a plan of measures to modernize the judiciary and the state apparatus, abandoning the obsolete and hindering functions of the market economy.

The second stage (1998-2002) at the 15th Congress of the Communist Party of China, a decision was made regarding the speech of the General Secretary of the Central Committee entitled "Building China-specific socialism in the 21st century by raising the banner of Dan Xiapin's theory." It is in the current era.

The idea was put forward that China can solve the prospect of the fate of socialism by combining Marxism and the reality of the present time.1 The party program of strengthening the state legislation and building a legal socialist state was developed as the main direction. The following tasks were set for the administrative reform of the administration:

- transformation of collective economic ministries and institutions into ministries and institutions that implement macroeconomic adjustment;
- re-organization of specially specialized economic ministries and institutions, reducing their number;
- strengthening the ministries and institutions that supervise and implement the implementation of laws.

The third stage (2002-2007) At the 16th Congress of the Communist Party of China, reform programs were adopted to adapt the legislation to market economy relations, and in the field of administrative management, to reduce the functions of the state apparatus and optimize their organizational structures. A way to encourage the development of the system of lower-level self-governing organizations of the Party was announced - to control the spending of tax revenues in the countryside. During this period, the rate of economic growth of China began to increase from 10.4 percent per year.

The fourth stage (started in 2007) focused the 17th Congress of the Communist Party on deepening the modernization of state and administrative organizations. Functions and some structures of the State Council, which develops the general strategic directions of the country based on the decisions of the Congress was shortened. Special attention was paid to the implementation of these reductions based on the policy of reducing state budgets. In the first years of the reforms, state budgets were reduced from 2000 to 400. As a result, many ministries and institutions were reduced. As a result of the reform of the State Council, only 29 of the 42 ministries were left, and 13 were reduced (ministries of coal industry, metallurgy, engineering, and prime minister). Ministries and institutions operating mainly in the field of macroeconomic coordination were left.

At the same time, the number of officials was also increased. For example, if there were 12 deputy ministers, now they have been reduced to 5. The ministerial staff was reduced by 15 percent, and civil servants at local government levels were reduced by 20 percent. By 2015, 2 million civil servants, or 25 percent of them, were cut.

Thus, reducing the number of employees of state management organizations at all levels, effective and optimal use of specialists and managers became one of the main directions of modernization in this area.1

After the reduction of a number of ministries and central institutions, new administrative structures were formed in the center and in the province, city, uyezd, and townships to align the state property. A system of vertical responsibility of the lower structures to the higher authorities was formed, and the legal basis was adopted for the upper level to be responsible to the State Council. The right of state agencies and structures to directly manage state property was taken away: now these rights were given to the enterprises, firms and companies themselves.

As a result of the modernization of state administration organizations, new management structures were formed at local levels: the main shareholder in several groups of several enterprises, companies were created and they exercised control over the disposal and use of property on behalf of the state; large associations of enterprises began to control specific areas of production; it was established that trade unions control some medium and small firms and enterprises.

The main goal of the modernization of public administration and service in China was to ensure the development of the market economy in the country, to adapt the public administration system to the requirements of the market economy, and to ensure that the administration creates favorable conditions for the development of business.

At the time of the beginning of the reforms - in the 90s of the 20th century, there were almost no private enterprises in China. Currently, they make up 75% of the total production. In China, the attitude not only to private ownership, but also to other areas of the economy has changed radically. Earlier, production and consumption were centralized, but now they have passed into the hands of firms and families. As a result of the carried out fundamental reforms, economic initiative, adaptation to the market, competition took the place of administrative control. Reforms in China proved that "freedom of individual initiatives is a factor of economic development" of famous economists in the world. The government decided to carry out comprehensive reforms not only in the industry, but also in the agrarian sector.

Despite having 7% of the world's arable land, China has to feed a quarter of the world's population. As a result of the development of production, the agricultural products distributed per capita have also increased. Reforms based on the principle of "practice is the criterion of truth" in villages and the use of scientific technology in agriculture, in turn, increased labor efficiency. It should be noted that in order to prevent the increase in unemployment that may occur as a result of the privatization of state- owned enterprises in China, the government decided to focus on enterprises. It was small business that made a great contribution to the adoption of innovative technologies by creating new jobs. In order to expand the State Small Business Financing Program, the government has been improving the legislation for economic development.

"Special state fund for the development of small and medium-sized businesses" was established in order to harmonize the market economy. This fund is fully financed from the state budget and acts as a catalyst for the development of small enterprises. The main purpose of this fund is to protect small business enterprises in the competition with large companies and to create an opportunity for them to fulfill their obligations.

At the same time, the economic modernization program for 2020-2050 was approved in China. According to him, the country's economy should be completely modernized by 2050. According to China's national economic development program, from 2006 to 2020, great importance is attached to the development of 11 branches of the economy.

A special agency - China Business Cooperation and Alignment Center was established to support small enterprises in the country and assist them in their technological cooperation with foreign companies and to manage this area. According to Chinese officials, there are currently about 5 million small business enterprises in the country. There are also more than 30 million private entrepreneurs.

On October 18-24, 2017, the 19th Congress of the Communist Party of China gained importance due to the fact that it was held at a crucial stage when China is entering a new era of socialism and building a society based on the middle class. According to the Chinese ambassador to Uzbekistan, Sun Lisze, "at the congress, the CPC and the country's achievements in recent years development strategies and programs were defined. As the world's second largest economic country and a major developing country, and a permanent member of the UN Security Council,

China plays an important role in the international arena, making a great contribution to the world economy and global development. That's why the syezd drew the attention of the whole world public."

At the Kurultoy, the results of China's five-year journey were evaluated. In the previous period, GDP increased by 7.2%, from 8 trillion US dollars to 12 trillion US dollars. China's contribution to world economic development increased by 30%.

13 million new jobs were created in the country, the real income of the population increased by 7.4%. More than 60 million people have been lifted out of poverty. In 2016, China's foreign trade turnover amounted to 3 trillion 680 billion US dollars.

The presentation of the following strategic plans in the speech of the Chinese leader helps to imagine the level of its modernization: "We will carry out these tasks in three stages: by 2020, to bring the society to a middle-income level; Focus on socialist modernization from 2020 to 2035; To turn our country into a rich, powerful, democratic, progressive, modern socialist country from 2035. From now until 2020, building a middle-class society will be a crucial task."

In his speech at the congress, Chinese President Xi Jinping announced a 14-point strategy for developing a Chinese model of socialism. In this place, first of all, the idea of "all for the people", fundamental changes, and innovation was discussed. It is also important to strengthen the foundations of the legal state, increase the welfare of the population, protect the environment, develop the concept of "one country - two systems", and strengthen global integration.

It can be seen that over the past 40 years in China, the modernization of public administration and service, its market economy adaptation to their relations, development of the market economy in all aspects of society, giving up the functions of state organizations to manage the society and strengthening the functions of its adaptation began to bear fruit. As a result of the transfer of management functions to the lowest management organizations, enterprises, firms and companies, the personal initiative of civil servants and employed people has increased. Evaluation of the administration based on the last results increased its responsibility to the population. In general, the formation of a unique Chinese model of public administration and service has become important. Asian, African and Latin American countries are currently interested in this model. Some countries are modernizing their public administration system based on China's experience.

Since the last quarter of the 20th century, fundamental reforms to update the Japanese public administration system have been implemented. When creating a management system that meets the requirements of the development of modern technologies, the leaders of the Japanese state paid significant attention to the modernization processes implemented in this field in Europe. The process of modernization of public administration in Japan was given great importance to be formed as a mixture of the classical concept of European managerialism and Japanese traditional management experience. In other words, Japanese experts deeply studied the experience of modernization of all public administration systems in European countries, and began to reconstruct the national experience in this field based on innovative ideas.

In Japan, the relationship between the legislature and the executive was mainly reformed in the second half of the 20th century. The legislative branch makes laws and the executive branch executes these laws. The Council of Ministers exercises executive power and is legally responsible to the Parliament. The Prime Minister is elected by the Parliament from among its deputies. House of Representatives and when the decision of the House of Advisers regarding the Prime Minister differs, as well as if the same opinion is not reached at the joint session held in accordance with the law, or if the House of Representatives does not approve the decision of the House of Advisers within 10 days, except for the time when the work of the Parliament is interrupted, the decision of the House of Representatives is considered the decision of the Parliament. Determines that the prime minister will be only among the members of the parliament.

It is also established that the House of Representatives has a superior position in solving the issue of the Prime Minister. The Prime Minister elected by the Parliament appoints the ministers of state. Interestingly, more than half of them should be appointed from among the deputies. The prime minister can also dismiss state ministers at his discretion. This system primarily leads to the cooperation of the legislative and executive powers. Also, the Prime Minister's power to dismiss ministers increases the accountability of ministers to the Prime Minister.

According to Article 65 of the Constitution of Japan, executive power is exercised by the Cabinet of Ministers, and based on this article, it is prohibited to establish an executive body operating independently of the Cabinet of Ministers. This prevents interference of the legislature and the judiciary in the affairs of the executive branch.

The prime minister and other state ministers, regardless of whether they are members of the chambers or not, can participate in the chamber meetings to express their opinion on the draft law at any time. They are also required to attend when requested by members of parliament to provide explanations and answers.

One of the important powers of the legislative power that limits or restrains the executive power is the Minister issuing a vote of no confidence or refusing to issue a resolution of confidence in the Court. According to Article 69 of the Constitution of Japan, if the House of Representatives passes a vote of no confidence in the Government or if the House of Representatives is not dissolved within 10 days after the rejection of the confidence resolution, the Cabinet of Ministers must announce a general resignation. Also, according to Article 7 of the Constitution of Japan, the Emperor has the authority to dissolve the House of Representatives on the advice and approval of the Government. Various approaches have been formed regarding the interpretation of this article of the Constitution. Representatives of the first approach believe that the power to dissolve the House of Representatives in Article 7 of the Constitution is established in Article 69 of the Constitution.

Representatives of the second approach believe that the power to dissolve the House of Representatives in Article 7 of the Constitution has the power to dissolve the Cabinet of Ministers in other cases, except for Article 69 of the Constitution. In order to find out the opinion of the people, it is necessary to hold elections before the due date.

In practice, in August 1952, Prime Minister Yoshida Huku decided to dissolve the House of Representatives under Article 7 of the Japanese Constitution even though there was no vote of no confidence in the Government. Against this, Mr. Tomabechi Yoshizou, a deputy of the House of Representatives at that time, appealed to the court to declare the dissolution invalid. This issue was brought up to the Supreme Court, which ultimately ended with the court refusing to consider such political issues based on the "state affairs theory".

The above legislative power and the executive power must restrain each other and maintain mutual balance mechanism to prevent abuse of power by branches of government or to limit the seizure of state power by one person or a group of persons. It is a pledge of the people's power and a reliable means of guaranteeing and protecting the rights and freedoms of the Japanese people stipulated in the Constitution.

In the researches of VG Khoros, a well-known Japanese scholar, the modernization of Japan is comparatively analyzed.

In Japan, the modernization of state power and local government organizations was carried out parallel to the reform of society. Modernization was first absorbed through the strong influence of traditional institutions and values of Western civilization: capitalist production developed under the leadership of patriarchal relations and the structure of firms as a "big family"; bourgeois democracy was formed in the spirit of traditional loyalty and reconciliation; the modern education system was strengthened by the Confucian tradition of examinations.

Also, the traditional Japanese civilization did not play the role of disseminating foreign and other cultural values, but brought the traditional national "community" into the capitalist structure as a full-fledged component of the socio-cultural combination. This situation became important and led to the "economic miracle" that ensured that Japan surpassed America and Europe in a number of areas.

Political scientists and sociologists have shown that the Japanese "economic miracle" depends on the specific characteristics of production processes, which are fundamentally different from the West, and that the Japanese model later spread to other countries of East Asia. Of course, initially in Japan, South Korea, Singapore, Taiwan and other Asian "dragons" and "tigers", structures and institutions similar to those in the West were created, but over time they began to operate based on different principles. If in the West, rational purposeful social action prevailed, then in Japan, valuable purposefulness prevailed.

From the point of view of modernization processes, Japan is the first among the late-developing countries to find solutions to the most difficult problems related to modernization. As a result of combining community and individualism, traditional corporatism and groupism, specific modernization processes were implemented. But in the course of modernization efforts in many "third world" countries, individualization destroyed traditional public structures, or, on the contrary, only modernization on the basis of the public (the so-called "non-capitalist way of development") did not give any results. Even today, people familiar with Japanese firms are surprised to see the atmosphere of patriarchal-corporate unity mentality focused on personal achievements and competition.

The development of ideological goals based on the principles of "Japanese spirit + foreign technology" in the 1970s and 1990s, and "Japanese spirit + Japanese technology" in the 1980s and their implementation show that the Japanese government adopted the European experience during the initial period of reforms in this field. , then began to enrich their national concepts based on this foreign experience.

As a result, a modern management system was created in Japan by the end of the 20th century, and a new management culture was formed accordingly. In this new system, the prospects of an advanced and developed world management culture are highlighted. The main aspect of this innovation is that it began to express long-term goals - strategic goals. This situation can be observed in every administrative office. In particular, the modernization of the business management system has been extremely accelerated: this system, in addition to targeting a long-term strategy, has entered into the system of market transactions and firmly esta In this process, "Forget today, think about tomorrow!" The slogan was contrasted with the western rule "If there is daylight, then there is food." This strategy, with its flexibility, quick adaptability, mobility and desire to find its place in the market, opened a wide path to the future, created opportunities for deep modernization in the field of management.

In general, the strategy of modernization of the Japanese public administration system is distinguished by its advance preparation for emerging events and problems.

That is why this road was briefly implemented under the slogan "Preparation for Events". In addition, the following description of the Japanese local and business management strategy was formed:

- adapting to changes;
- adapting to the environment and the area where it is located;
- to take into account all opportunities for development in the fast- changing world, not for a specific time frame, but for the long term and to use them effectively;
- development of technical, technological and social factors acceptance as the main resources of development, etc

Although the Japanese are historically and naturally considered to be clear thinkers about events, they have effectively assimilated the demands of conceptual developments in Japan and advanced to the level of foresight.

Japan's new management system focused on the following four main functions: 1) planning; 2) organization; 3) encouragement; 4) control. These are the most important factors finding and mastering them became the basis for success in this field. In particular, the newly formed science of personnel management played an important role in this process. That is why one of the famous founders of management management, the American scientist William Ouchi, classified the Japanese management system not only on the basis of Western experience, but as a collection of spiritual and cultural benefits that originate from the uniqueness of the Japanese nation and are gathered in a natural way.

One of the most important features of the Japanese management system is the human factor at the center of Japanese management. The Japanese management system and production traditions consist of the most modern, scientific social technologies, which encourage people to work and effectively organize their behavior within the group. In this field, the Japanese were initially students, but by the present time they have become teachers and are serving as an example to the whole world.

By the end of the 20th century, the main aspects of the Japanese management model and management culture began to be explained by the following:

- long- term strategy;
- continuity in the formation of innovative management culture;
- rapid assimilation of the latest examples of world technology and technical culture;

- view the development and modernization of the human factor and work with the general staff as promising resources;
- preservation of national cultural standards, their support and increase.

There are often views that economic and legal knowledge is enough for the formation of social management culture. In history, that is, in the 30s of the 20th century a "great depression or system" that gripped the western world.

After the world crisis, such an understanding of social management was put to an end. At that time, the President of the United States, Franklin Delano Roosevelt, in his address to the governors of the states in the White House, said the following words: "The preservation of our national wealth is only one part of the question of national labor productivity. What does the concept of "national labor productivity" mean? First of all, it means the reflection of the management of the "human resource" as a human activity".

Since the 1930s, the concept of "good education" has been firmly rooted in the reflection of acquisition of various fields of knowledge: from sociology, political science, spirituality, history, psychology and other complex systems theory to informatics, logic, mathematics, prediction technology, and knowledge began to gain importance. From this period, the culture of management began to appear as a collection of multi-science, management began to understand the use of information from a number of disciplines, their latest achievements, and turning integrated information into the language of management decision-making.

Therefore, representatives of various scientific fields began to participate in the field of management, and secondly, it became legal to develop the science of management personnel on the basis of constant retraining of management employees and civil servants, continuous updating of their acquired knowledge.

Foreign experts have formed a fascinating view of Japanese domestic and business management: how did the Japanese manage to achieve extremely high quality products using technology, equipment and raw materials used in Europe and the United States? According to the opinion of Japanese experts, "the quality of the product is increased not by equipment or machines, but by people, of course foreigners should understand this."

Leaders of Japanese enterprises and management organizations have been trying to find the secret to harnessing human resources and effectively using their potential. Of course, by the present time, these secrets have been discovered, and they have dramatically increased the effectiveness of well-educated and talented organizational leaders and manag It is known that management managers in developed countries are trained by special secondary and higher educational institutions, state- owned and private schools, lyceums and colleges. This profession requires such a high degree of diligence that the Germans jokingly called the state of stress, which causes mental exhaustion as a result of excessive stress, "manager's disease".

Each country has certain limits on the number of managers. They are the "golden fund of the nation". Among the socio-psychological qualities of the owners of this profession, the researchers show that initiative and high work ability are the most important. Among them, the main ones are creative thinking, strategic thinking, the ability to unite the strength of many people, and the tendency to innovate.

The main difference between a traditional manager and a modern manager is that a modern manager not only maintains the current order in the organization, performs general control, but also introduces innovations into management, further develops the current order, and inspires them based on gaining people's trust.

True, there is a lot of management literature in the West. Of course, it appeared as a response to the demand of market relations. Therefore, in most literature, it is noted that there is a great need for managers who are able to innovate, fight hard in the market and win the competition. Of course, this raises the question of what managers and managers should pay attention to when preparing to solve traditional and innovative issues of management.

Management staff cannot compete with modern managers in achieving their goal, i.e. occupying an important place in the management culture, with the employees under their management by means of operating on the basis of the principles of organizational culture. Organizational culture is a system of customs and traditions that take into account formal and informal laws and norms of management activity, individual interests, individual behavior of each employee in the existing organization, the development of managerial work style, the growth of employee goals, and the system of customs and traditions formed in the field of supervision.

Acting on the control system is, first of all, an echo response to the influences of the internal and external environment. Based on the nature of the organization, the management method is determined. For example, if the state of the organization's environment and technologies are in harmony, the goals are defined, and people are able to do things voluntarily, then the traditional method of management is very suitable for such a task. At the same time, for the development of the management system, initiative, application of innovative ideas, managers' worldview and skills improvement are needed. In Japanese social management, the ability to respond to this need is a factor in ensuring that management is extremely effective.

Japanese scientist A. Khakamada, connecting the management of different regions to the state of society, expressed the following opinion: "In the West, people are like bricks, from which a certain society can be built; In Japan, in Asia, people are like clay, they lose their shape in political changes; And in Russia, people are like sand. If the form (that is, the state) is removed, they will be scattered like sand". It can be seen from the ideas that the state administration is the modern role of the national mentality is also important in nationalization. This situation was formed as a result of Japan's desire to become a strong state and empire in the first half of the 20th century, its defeat had a strong impact on the people's psyche, and the nation's natural desire to unite around the government in order to restore its leading position in the world. Therefore, the Japanese people have developed a feeling of accepting the government's activities as their own. These factors played an important role in the modernization of state administration.

The following is the personnel management system in Japan distinctive features:

1.   "Lifetime employment" system. According to him, lifelong employment is not an official right, but a tradition. This concept represents the relationship between the employer and the employee as a way of thinking. For example, an enterprise or organization undertakes not to reduce employees even if its income decreases. Japanese managers like employees who are development oriented and live with strategic ideas. In the Japanese management system, giving more perspectives has led to the development of a form of employment for life. This type of employment makes employees feel the stability of their life from the very beginning of their work. His match retires at the age of 55 (60 years in some companies).

2.   Age is the principle of greatness. In the Japanese spiritual world, the wisdom of the elderly is highly valued. For this reason, the

principle of seniority is followed in the personnel management system. Based on this principle, older people are paid more due to the fact that they have more work experience and respect for their age. For example, a 25-year-old employee is 2.5 times more likely to be assigned to long-term service than a 20-year-old employee. Also, paying attention to seniority plays the role of motivating them to work effectively. The employee's salary has been growing consistently over the years.

This situation helps to effectively align the labor force in the management of Japanese enterprises and businesses, and eliminates the unemployment of the labor force.

Emphasis is placed on, the corporate spirit in Japanese state and local government and business administration. "Corporate spirit" means imbuing employees with feelings of loyalty and commitment to the ideals of the organization, enterprise or firm. Each enterprise or organization has its own uniform, slogan, anthem, and traditions of holding various events. When a new employee wears the uniform of the company, he begins to feel like a different person, he is influenced by the spirit of responsibility for self-discipline. Feelings of pride and self-confidence begin to shine in an employee who feels the badges of Matsusito or Sumimoto companies on his clothes.

In Japan, every enterprise or organization spends a certain amount of money, organizes various recreation and entertainment activities to keep the morale of its employees at a high level. Of course, all expenses are covered by the active and diligent work of the labor team. In Japanese society, unlike in the West, the collective spirit is much stronger. 2

In Japan, industry and production mainly consist of private and non-state forms of ownership, and the conceptual strategic task of human resource management in their enterprises, organizations and firms for several decades and instructions were developing. Western and national characteristics have left their mark on them. The results of development and national identity in this area can be seen in Table 1 below:

Table 1

Strategy	Conceptual guidelines	Methods
effective use of "Human factor" in	The system of lifetime	to climb up with the ranks of the service

management	employment; motivated spiritual-meaning	(the principle of "glorifying the elders");
	The possibility of integration of personnel and personnel interchangeably;	complex system of Performance evaluation; horizontally exchange retraining in a regular manner based on the principle;
		to pay more attention to recruitment system;
		development based on group method of work;
		The advanced system of HR 'top-down';
		Practice consultation when making decisions (grouping);
		A developed system of interactions and communications;
		Leveling social differences between managers and ordinary employees from the outside;

Another important feature of Japanese governance is its highly ideological nature. On the one hand, the mechanism of ideology is the core of management, it repeatedly develops and comprehensively supports the Japanese type of management. On the other hand, maf struggle provides vitality to the effective functioning of Japanese administration. The main goal of ideological influence on the employee is to awaken his natural love for the company where he works as a family. Also, another direction of ideological work is aimed at raising the feelings of patriotism and feeling national pride. That is why Japan is developing further as a leading country in the world in all fields.

CONTROL QUESTIONS

1. What does the Chinese model of modernization of the state management system include?
2. What are the characteristics of administrative reforms in China?
3. A fundamental reform to update the Japanese public administration system? What do hots include?

7-THEME: THE PRINCIPLE OF DIVISION OF STATE POWER IN UZBEKISTAN AND REFORMS TO ENSURE MUTUAL BALANCE

Plan:

1. Main functions of public receptions and virtual receptions.
2. Modernization of the system of state authorities.
3. Measures to further reform the judicial system, strengthen the guarantees of reliable protection of the rights and freedoms of citizens.

A new stage of the process of modernization of state authorities in Uzbekistan began when Shavkat Mirziyoyev began to perform the duties of the head of state - the President in September 2016. As the main principle of modernization, the idea of "State agencies should serve our people, not the people to the state agencies" was put forward. 2017 was announced as the "Year of Communication with the People and Human Interests". However, it was necessary to determine the state of the administration of the state authorities in the country, and the opinion of the citizens about it. Bitter experiences that the reforms started without consulting the people's opinion never corresponded to the principles of justice required the implementation of measures that have not yet been seen in the history of On December 28, 2016, the President of the Republic of Uzbekistan "With appeals of natural and legal entities decree on measures to fundamentally improve the work system" was announced. According to it, the People's Reception of the President of the Republic of Uzbekistan and the Virtual Reception of the President of the Republic of Uzbekistan were created in the Republic of Karakalpakstan, regions and Tashkent, as well as in each district and city (except the cities subordinate to the district) on the basis of the Citizens' Reception of the Affairs Department of the Office of the President of the Republic of Uzbekistan.

According to this decree, the following are defined as the main tasks of public receptions and virtual receptions:

- to organize direct dialogue with the population, to ensure the functioning of a qualitatively new and effective system of working with appeals of individuals and legal entities, aimed at fully protecting the rights and freedoms and legal interests of natural and legal entities; - citizens to the President of the Republic of Uzbekistan, unconditional implementation of constitutional rights to appeal to the Oliy Majlis, the Office of the President of the Republic of Uzbekistan, authority, state administration organizations, courts, law enforcement and control organizations, local state authorities, other state organizations (hereinafter - state organizations) and economic management organizations create conditions for its increase;

- implementation of systematic monitoring and control over the consideration of appeals received by public receptions and Virtual receptions and sent to state organizations and economic supervision organizations; - conducting receptions of individuals and representatives of legal entities with the participation of officials of state organizations and economic management organizations, including via video conference;

- Monitoring of registration, summarization, systematization and review of appeals to public receptions and Virtual Reception wide use of modern information and communication technologies in working with appeals by introducing and maintaining a single electronic information system".

President Shavkat Mirziyoyev, in his speech at the ceremonial ceremony dedicated to the 24th anniversary of the adoption of the Constitution of the Republic of Uzbekistan, clearly revealed the disconnection of relations between the government authorities and the people, and the fact that the management system has moved away from the interests of the people and solving their problems. He gave the following evidence about this: "We forgot to communicate with people later. Entering into them, talking openly and sincerely, listening to their pain, unfortunately fell to the last place in our activities. What do people want from government agencies these days? Speaking of this, I would like to draw your attention to an important issue... I must say frankly, a lot has become clear from the analysis of these appeals. So to speak, they opened our eyes to the acute problems that exist in our lives. Here's what people are referring to.

First of all, they are appealing for removal of bureaucratic obstacles in various fields, cancellation of many departmental instructions that are against the law, allocation of bank loans with optimal rate, termination of illegal audits on activity, activity of law enforcement agencies.

At the same time, many requests are received from our residents regarding the improvement of housing construction, utility, transport and trade services, energy supply, and the condition of roads.

You see, dear friends, all these demands are legal and fair. I don't think there is any need to comment on this. But here a question arises: wasn't it necessary for local governments and agencies, relevant officials to solve the vital problems raised in these appeals in time?

Now, with your permission, let me dwell on the most urgent and priority tasks in this regard. First of all, based on the main goals and tasks of the "Year of Communication with the People and Human Interests", it is necessary to fundamentally revise the approach to the interaction of state organizations with citizens. In this regard, we need to constantly communicate with the population, introduce new mechanisms and effective methods of solving the problems that are bothering them. We are thinking about transitioning to a qualitatively new system of working with people in the activities of state agencies, which the population appeals to the most"[19] It can be seen that the report set the goal of making serious and drastic changes in the system of state authorities. In this area, the idea of implementing the process of modernization, which covers the management system in depth and the path followed by the western countries, was put forward. In a short period of time - in 10 months, i.e. on July 21, 2017, one million appeals were received at People's reception centers. Even in the history of Western countries, institutions that collect information on

---

[19] [1] *Mirziyoyev Sh.M.* Ensuring the rule of law and human interests is a guarantee of the country's development and people's well-being: speech at the solemn ceremony dedicated to the 24th anniversary of the adoption of the Constitution of the Republic of Uzbekistan (December 7, 2016) Volume 1. - T.: "Uzbekistan", 2017. - P.114-115.

people's problems on this scale and analyze them are not found. At the same time, the mechanism that not a single one of the appeals is left out of the attention of state organizations has shown its effectiveness. 97,504 of the appeals received within 10 months were for housing, 56,567 for employment, 33,813 for civil cases in courts, 28,864 for financial assistance to the family, 27,956 for executive documents on the collection of alimony, 17,582 for child allowance, 16,567 were related to labor and employment issues, 15,743 were related to criminal proceedings in courts, 15,728 were related to citizenship passport issues, and 14,491 were related to issues such as conversion (except for business)[20].

As it can be seen from the distribution of appeals by sectors, it is clear that the activities of the state government in all directions deviated from the principles of ensuring human rights and freedoms and working on the basis of the interests of the people. In particular, it became clear that the population's housing and employment problems have become too much. It is important that the higher authorities of the state managed to obtain complete information about the inefficient management services of the network and lower state authorities. The analysis clearly showed that the funds allocated from the state budget to state authorities are underinvested, and their ability to provide public services to the population has decreased. This situation demanded to start the process of modernization of the system of state authorities without delay.

The head of state and the government took the path of comprehensive modernization of the system of state authorities. The following modernization directions have been implemented in this area since September 2016:

1) According to the Decree of the President of the Republic of Uzbekistan "On Free Economic Zones", uniform legal conditions were created for all three free economic zones in Uzbekistan (Navoi, Angren and Jizzakh). Equalization of taxes, duties and other benefits created favorable conditions for foreign companies. Companies operating in these economic zones were exempted from taxes and customs duties. Privileges were granted for periods of 3-10 years depending on the size of investments: from 300 thousand to 3 million dollars - for a period of 3 years, from 3 million to 5

---

[20] See: virtual lobby of the President of the Republic of Uzbekistan// https://pm.gov.uz.

million dollars - for a period of 5 years, from 5 million to 10 million dollars - for a period of 7 years.

2) Supplement for development of state entrepreneurship, protection of private property, improvement of business environment decided to take measures. In particular, from January 1, 2017, all types of inspections of business entities were canceled. The Business Ombudsman Institute was established to strengthen parliamentary control over the implementation of laws on business rights and interests. In order to further increase the quality and transparency of the provision of state services to business entities, the possibilities of their use, to strengthen the guarantees of protection of the rights and legal interests of entrepreneurs, and to ensure the effectiveness of direct communication with the people on the ground, the President of the Republic of Uzbekistan on

February 1, 2017 "State services to business entities" Decision on additional measures to improve display mechanisms" was adopted. Laws of the Republic of Uzbekistan "On Combating Corruption" (January 4, 2017) and "On Public Control" (April 12, 2018) typical of developed countries were adopted; 3) A 5-year privatization program has been adopted, according to which the assets of more than 1,200 companies are being offered to foreign investors. The main goal was to reduce the share of the state in the economy by increasing the private sector. In addition, foreign investors are offered 900 new investment projects worth 41 billion soums in the fields of oil and gas, petrochemicals, textiles, food, pharmaceuticals and construction materials;

4) 15 countries - Australia, Austria, Great Britain, Germany, Denmark, Spain, Italy, Canada, Luxembourg, Netherlands, Republic of Korea, Singapore, Finland, Switzerland and Japan, 12 other countries from April 1, 2017 - The visa regime for tourists- citizens of Belgium, Indonesia, PRC, Malaysia, USA, France, Vietnam, Israel, Poland, Hungary, Portugal and the Czech Republic who have reached the age of 55 has been canceled;

5) On September 2, 2017, the Decree of the President of the Republic of Uzbekistan "On the first measures to liberalize the currency policy" was signed. This Decree initiated a new stage of development of the business sector in the country and development of international economic relations.[21]

As a result of the adoption of the legal basis for the development of economy and investments, the state administration began to adapt to the laws

---

[21] See: Mirziyoyeva's reform in Uzbekistan - a new course for freedom of speech? 18.12.2016. // http: // www.dialog.tj/news/.

of the market economy. In this area, more enterprises and companies have been enabled to manage themselves independently and based on the requirements of the market economy. These changes mean not only the beginning of economic development in the country, but also the beginning of the process of modernization in the field of public administration.

The processes of implementing the Strategy of Actions on the five priority directions of the development of the Republic of Uzbekistan in 2017-2021 began to bear results in a short period of time. Adoption of the State Program for implementation in 2017 - "Year of Communication with the People and Human Interests" was the first mechanism for the practical realization of the priorities of strategic development. In the first year, the partnership of state organizations and institutions of civil society aimed at the effective implementation of this State program, including the participation of foreign specialists and international experts in this field, began to bear fruit. Until August 15, 2017, 15 laws and more than 700 other normative legal documents aimed at the development of all spheres of state and community life were adopted in connection with the implementation of the Action Strategy. In particular, taking into account modern requirements and priorities in the field of improving the system of state and community construction, what are the structures, tasks and functions of 16 ministries, departments and other organizations were reviewed, 20 state and economic management organizations, other organizations were reorganized.

The judicial system has been fundamentally revised. The Supreme Court of the Republic of Uzbekistan, the only supreme body of the judiciary, administrative courts authorized to consider administrative disputes arising from public-legal relations, as well as cases of administrative violations, was established. The system of internal affairs organizations was reformed, and their main activity was directed to ensuring the rights, freedoms and legal interests of citizens - "Serving the interests of the people".

In the field of economic development and liberalization, the tax system was reformed, tax holidays were provided to honest taxpayers - business entities. Within the framework of regional socio-economic development programs, 13,339 projects were implemented, 2.1 trillion soums of credit were used, 10 free economic zones, 5 small industrial zones were established. 22 "roadmaps" were approved with the European Union and

21 foreign countries in trade-economic, investment, technology and financial-technical fields.[22]

President Sh.M. Mirziyoyev, as the head of state, began his initial activity with reforms aimed at improving the socio-economic conditions of entrepreneurs and owners. It was noted that the main strategic goal of the state is the civil society, and the social and economic support of this society is the layer of owners. Also, the state's policy of transition to a market economy necessitated the task of liberating the owners' stratum and liberating the economy. In addition, the owners are also the financial basis for the implementation of the state's social policy in the market economy would be implemented in exchange for creating new jobs, creating economic production infrastructure, and increasing the state budget through taxes. Therefore, on October 5, 2016, the President of the Republic of Uzbekistan Sh. M. Mirziyoyev adopted the Decree "On additional measures to ensure the rapid development of business activities, comprehensive protection of private property and qualitative improvement of the business environment."

Special emphasis was placed on limiting government interference in the economy, that is, on freeing the activities of entrepreneurs. In this regard, the following was determined:

State organizations, first of all, law enforcement and control structures:

- ensure the unconditional implementation of the above-mentioned requirement and the priority of the rights and legal interests of the event subjects in their activities;
- on the basis of a critical analysis of their duties and powers, they should submit within two months, in accordance with the established procedure, proposals to improve the measures for the prevention, prevention and prevention of violations and to increase their efficiency;
- to ensure the strict implementation of the requirements of the legal documents on the liability of officials for illegal interference and obstruction of business activities, and for unjustified interruption of their activities, as well as the recovery of damages caused to business entities directly from the culprits.

It should be noted that starting from January 1, 2017:

- all types of unscheduled inspections of business entities

---

[22] Decree of the President of the Republic of Uzbekistan dated August 15, 2017 No. F-5024 "On measures for further implementation of the strategy of actions in the five priority areas of development of the Republic of Uzbekistan in 2017-2021" // http://www.press- service.uz.

are canceled, when legal entities are being liquidated, as well as on the basis of appeals made by individuals and legal entities in cases of violation of the legislation with the exception of short-term inspections conducted according to the decision of the Public Council;

- all types of alternative inspections of the activities of business entities, including criminal cases, will be canceled;

- business entities and their employees who have committed violations for the first time in the implementation of financial and economic activities are exempted from administrative and criminal liability in the event that they voluntarily eliminate the violations within the time limits specified by law and compensate for the material damage caused (with the exception of cases of damage to human health and life) , are exempted from the application of fines and financial sanctions (except fines);

- persons who have committed offenses related to the implementation of illegal business activities for the first time shall be released from administrative and criminal liability if they voluntarily compensate for the damage, register as a joint venture subject, and issue the necessary permitting documents within one month from the date of detection of the offense;

- criminal punishment in the form of deprivation of the right to carry out business activities shall not be applied to business entities.[23]

Of course, the head of state planned to start reforms to reorganize the economy on the basis of market relations, and then to adapt the state executive power and its structures accordingly. In other words, this was the first, but the main step towards the modernization of the executive power system. Besides, this country for the first time in its history, it was a decisive measure to sharply limit the powers of state management and law enforcement agencies.

Soon after, on May 5, 2017, the Decree of the President of the Republic of Uzbekistan "On the establishment of the representative institute for the protection of the rights and legal interests of business entities under the President of the Republic of Uzbekistan" was adopted. According to the decree, a representative for the protection of the rights and legal interests of business entities (here in after the Representative) was established under the President of the Republic of Uzbekistan. It is assumed that this institute will

---

[23] Decree of the President of the Republic of Uzbekistan "On additional measures to ensure the rapid development of business activities, comprehensive protection of private property and qualitative improvement of the business environment". October 5, 2016.// http://www.press-servis.uz/uz/ document/5340/.

serve to introduce new mechanisms of effective communication between business entities and state organizations, to create additional guarantees of state protection aimed at ensuring their rights and legal interests.

By decree, the Representative shall participate in the formation and implementation of the state policy in this area, control over the observance of the rights and legal interests of business entities, and provide legal support to business entities when their activities are being investigated. Also, it studies whether the norms and requirements of legal documents in the field are being implemented in practice, evaluates their impact on the implementation of business activities, prepares proposals for improving the legislation aimed at strengthening the legal guarantees of entrepreneurship and stimulating their development. The representative exercises his powers independently and not subordinate to state organizations and their officials.[24]

The President focused this institute mainly on the development of medium and small businesses in the country, freeing them from various bureaucratic obstacles, protecting the rights of owners, and improving the legal framework in this field. As this change is one of the measures to increase the efficiency of public administration, it was focused on increasing the efficiency of public service. In other words, it was expressed as the beginning of the modernization of the state executive power.

The President's reform on the modernization of the executive power system was expressed in the Decree of the President of the Republic of Uzbekistan "On measures to further reform the judicial system and strengthen the guarantees of reliable protection of the rights and freedoms of citizens" (October 21, 2016). The main reason for this is that the executive power and its local structures have overreached their powers, or they have eliminated bureaucratic methods in their work, which was connected with the strengthening of the judicial power.

Because the citizen who suffered from the administration could defend himself only when he applied to the court, which is not subject to the executive power. And the decisions of the judicial power should not allow the executive power to abuse its powers. That is why the President's Decree "On measures to further reform the judicial system, strengthen the guarantees of reliable protection of the rights and freedoms of citizens" states "to

---

[24] Decree of the President of the Republic of Uzbekistan "On the establishment of the representative institute under the President of the Republic of Uzbekistan for the protection of the rights and legal interests of business entities". May 5, 2017.// http://www.press-service.uz/uz/lists/view/470.

improve the efficiency of the activity of courts, law enforcement and control organizations, to increase the public's confidence in justice, In order to ensure the rule of law in society and strengthen legality, the following main priorities of the state policy in the field of further reform of the judicial system were determined:

- to the norms of the Constitution on the independence of the judiciary and to the activities of the administration of justice ensure that the principle of inevitability of responsibility for interference is followed without deviation;
- to take necessary measures immediately in relation to cases of encroachment on the rights, freedoms and legal interests of citizens;
- timely resolution of appeals of individuals and legal entities, ensuring the inevitability of criminal liability for allowing situations of indifference and indifference in the consideration of appeals, as well as taking all necessary measures to restore violated rights;
- ensuring openness and transparency of activities, wide use of effective mechanisms of cooperation with institutions of civil society, mass media and population;
- planning and organizing activities based on a comprehensive analysis of the results of the work, focusing primarily on identifying and eliminating the causes and conditions of systemic violations by improving the practice of law enforcement and existing legislation;

- to strengthen departmental control over the prevention, prevention and control of abuse and other offenses among employees, to ensure strict compliance with the rules of etiquette;

- to ensure unconditional observance of the rights and legal interests of citizens, to introduce advanced scientific and technical tools and information and communication technologies aimed at increasing the efficiency of activities, as well as modern forms and methods of work organization.

Also under the President of the Republic of Uzbekistan The highest qualification commission for the selection and recommendation of judges, the Supreme Court of the Republic of Uzbekistan, the Supreme Economic Court, the Prosecutor General's Office and the Ministry of Justice for the first time for a period of five years and it was proposed to create the legal basis for appointment (election) for a period of time, and then for an indefinite period.[25]

Soon after, on February 22, 2017, the Decree of the President of the Republic of Uzbekistan "On measures to fundamentally improve the structure of the judicial system of the Republic of Uzbekistan and increase the effectiveness of its activities" was adopted.

In accordance with the decree, the Supreme Council of Judges of the Republic of Uzbekistan was established in order to fundamentally improve the system of selection of candidates and appointment to judicial positions, to expand the participation of judges in this process, and to increase the status and powers of the body responsible for the formation of a highly qualified corps of judges.

To form a corps of judges for the Supreme Council of Judges based on an open and fair selection of qualified experts for judicial positions, to take measures to prevent violation of the integrity of judges and interference in their activities in the implementation of justice, to organize professional training of candidates and judges, to initiate dialogue with the population tasks have been assigned.

The Supreme Council of Judges has been given powers to appoint and dismiss all judges in agreement with the President of the Republic of Uzbekistan, except for the judges of the Constitutional Court of the Republic of Uzbekistan, the Supreme Court, the Military Court of the Republic of Uzbekistan, the Republic of Karakalpakstan, the presidents of the regional and Tashkent city courts.

Another important aspect of the decree is that the Supreme Court of Uzbekistan Res publications and the Supreme Economic Court are the only supreme body of judicial power in the field of civil, criminal, administrative and economic court work - the Supreme Court of the Republic of Uzbekistan was merged. This reform led to the elimination of

---

[25] Decree of the President of the Republic of Uzbekistan "On measures to further reform the judicial system, strengthen the guarantees of reliable protection of the rights and freedoms of citizens". October 21, 2016.// http://www.press-service.uz/uz/lists/view/40.

overlapping functions in the management of the judicial system and the formation of a unified judicial practice.

Administrative Court of the Supreme Court of the Republic of Uzbekistan, administrative courts of the Republic of Karakalpakstan, regions and Tashkent city, district (city) serving to ensure the implementation of constitutional guarantees of the right of citizens to appeal to the court against the illegal actions (inaction) of state organizations and their officials for the first time administrative courts were established.

Based on the modern requirements, as well as in order to further improve the system of protection of the rights of business subjects, the economic courts of the Republic of Karakalpakstan, regions and the city of Tashkent were changed into relevant economic courts. Taking into account the economic potential of the country and the growth of business entities, inter-district and district (city) economic courts were established. In general, the location of established administrative and economic courts increased the level of access to judicial protection of citizens living in remote areas, including entrepreneurs.[26]

Action strategy on the five priority areas of further development of the Republic of Uzbekistan: "deepening democratic reforms aimed at improving the state and society and strengthening the role of parliament and political parties in the modernization of the country, reforming the public administration system, developing the organizational and legal foundations of public service, "Electronic improvement of the "government" system, quality of public services and the main goal of promoting the tasks of "increasing the efficiency, implementing public control mechanisms, strengthening the role of civil society institutions and mass media" is to popularize the working methods of state management organizations and the content and essence of their implementation, to popularize the main directions of state policy. to increase the welfare of the

---

[26] Decree of the President of the Republic of Uzbekistan "On measures to fundamentally improve the structure of the judicial system of the Republic of Uzbekistan and increase the effectiveness of its activities" February 22, 2017// http://www.press-service.uz/en/lists/view/261

people, to raise the economic and social potential of the country to a high level.

CONTROL QUESTIONS

1. What are the main tasks of Public Reception and Virtual Reception?
2. What does the modernization of the system of state authorities include?
3. What are the measures to further reform the judicial system, strengthen the guarantees of reliable protection of the rights and freedoms of citizens?

8- THEME: MODERNIZATION OF THE EXECUTIVE POWER SYSTEM IN UZBEKISTAN
Plan:

1. Issues of further improvement of the neighborhood institution.
2. To fundamentally improve the efficiency of the internal affairs organizations.
3. Improving the management system in the field of foreign trade.

Modernization of state power organizations in the country, especially the executive power system, initially began with the preparation of conditions for self-management organizations to reach the level of functioning based on the requirements of civil society institutions. Because the reform of government organizations – ministries, state committees and other state agencies and institutions, the lowest level of local government – self-management, required the development of their financial and other resources.

The Decree of the President of the Republic of Uzbekistan on February 3, 2017 "On Measures to Further Improve Neighborhood Institutions" aims to modernize the self-governing organizations in the country, to make them not as "objects of subordination", but cooperation in their relations with local executive power structures. it was focused on not being available as an organization. The priority directions for further improvement of the following neighborhood institutions were defined in the decree:

- strengthening the place and role of citizens' self-government organizations in society, turning them into real experts and helpers of the people;

- to further increase theimportance and prestige of neighborhoods in the formation of an atmosphere of mutual respect, kindness and solidarity, preservation and development of national and universal values in our society;

- strengthening the mutual cooperation of citizens' self-government organizations with state and non-state external agencies in order to educate young people to be spiritually rich and physically healthy, to ensure their employment, to protect the young generation from ideological threats, to provide social support to the needy segments of the population, representatives of the elderly generation;

- to expand the direct participation of neighborhoods in ensuring public order and security, early prevention of crimes, strengthening citizens' sense of respect for the law;

- introduction of effective mechanisms for protecting the rights and legal interests of citizens' self-governing organizations and coordinating their activities, ensuring the practice of applying uniform rights in the neighborhood system.

According to the decree, the republican council for coordinating the activities of citizens' self-government organizations was established in the form of an association of citizens' assemblies, giving it the status of a legal entity. Also, the task of organizing the councils established in the Republic of Karakalpakstan, regions and Tashkent city, districts and cities as constituent structures of the Republican Council was determined. Prime Minister of the Republic of Uzbekistan, Chairman of the Dzhokorgi Council of the Republic of Karakalpakstan, Regions, Tashkent city for the purpose of increasing the authority and status of the councils, bringing the issues raised by the local population to the attention of the leaders of the executive authorities and further expanding their direct participation in solving issues: district and city mayors were assigned the task of presiding over the Republican Council and territorial councils on a public basis.

In order to effectively ensure the performance of the tasks assigned to the councils, to strengthen the material and technical base of the activities of citizens' self-government organizations, and to increase the efficiency of the work on the financing of socio-economic programs implemented in the field, the first deputies of the chairmen of the Republican Council and regional councils at the same time launched the "Mahalla" fund. The initiative to preside over the relevant republic administration and regional departments and divisions was supported.

Also, in order to further increase the efficiency of the measures implemented in the Republic Council on organizational affairs and methodological issues, in order to further increase the effectiveness of the measures implemented in the areas regarding the love of the Motherland, respect for the centuries-old traditions of our people, ensuring peace and tranquility in the neighborhoods, and supporting the social activity of the representatives of the older generation, the Decree the deputy chairman, as well as the positions of the deputy chairman for youth affairs, religious-educational issues, the elderly and veterans' affairs in the Republican Council and regional councils, and the deputy chairman of the neighborhood assembly of citizens, which operates on a public basis, in the organizations of self-management of citizens - for youth issues it was envisaged to introduce the position of cons In order to ensure the effective performance of the tasks entrusted to the self-governing organizations of citizens, the Council of the neighborhood assembly includes the deputies of the chairman of the assembly of citizens (advisers of the chairman of the assembly of citizens on the affairs of the elderly and veterans and youth issues), prevention inspectors in the area, educational institutions and rural medical centers (family polyclinics) and about their activities.

It was decided to introduce the practice of submitting reports to the assembly of citizens (the assembly of citizens' representatives) every quarter.[27]

This Decree has become important as a legal basis for self-governing organizations to operate based on the interests of the population, to solve problems arising in their places of residence in cooperation with local executive state authorities, to independently perform some of their functions and powers, and to increase the social activity of the population. In the Decree of the President of the Republic of Uzbekistan on February 14, 2017 "On measures to further improve the traffic management system", it is stated that "the formation of an effective system of traffic management based on an integrated approach to the process of designing, building and using automobile roads and artificial structures, the legal basis for creating a full-fledged customer service, which allows to improve the financing system, design and improve the quality of road construction works, has been created.

Management in this field was previously carried out by the company, but now it has been given the status of a state committee as a single state auditor.[28]

---

[27] Decree of the President of the Republic of Uzbekistan "On measures to further improve the neighborhood institute". February 3, 2017.// http://www.press-service.uz/uz/lists/view/228.

Its role as an executive authority has been increased, and opportunities have been created to coordinate road management in the republic from a single center.

In the Decree of the President of the Republic of Uzbekistan on February 16, 2017 "On measures to further improve the management system in the field of culture and sports", "the existing state management system is a comprehensive solution to the problems of the development of culture and sports, as well as, it does not allow to fully ensure the effective implementation of state policy in these areas, despite the breadth and importance of the tasks undertaken by them, the Ministry of Culture and Sports does not ensure active cooperation with state administration organizations and local authorities, and its activities are often cultural-negative situations such as the fact that it is limited to the holding of public and sports events" were highlighted, and it was pointed out that it is necessary to adapt Uzbekistan to the system of a separate ministry for sports affairs, which is raising its prestige in the world.

On the basis of this Decree "The Ministry of Culture and Sports Affairs of the Republic of Uzbekistan was abolished and on its basis: the Ministry of Culture of the Republic of Uzbekistan and the State Committee of Physical Education and Sports of the Republic of Uzbekistan were established. The division of the spheres, which are sharply different from each other by their important features, into two separate spheres (into the ministry and the state committee), in addition to increasing the effectiveness of the management system, began to ensure the more rapid development of the sphere of culture and sports. In particular, as a task of the State Committee for Physical Education and Sports, "together with local government organizations, citizens' self-management organizations, physical education and sports societies, educational institutions, public organizations, the population, especially young people, women, the elderly, rural As a result of setting such urgent issues as organizing large-scale work on the popularization of sports and physical education among the population, mass sports events in cities and districts, national games and competitions in national sports"[29], within the next year, sports

---

[28] Decree of the President of the Republic of Uzbekistan "On measures to further improve the traffic management system". February 14, 2017.
//http://www.press-service.uz/uz/lists/view/256

[29] 2017 of the President of the Republic of Uzbekistan. Decree "On further improvement of the management system in the field of culture and sports",

equipment, fields and its modern species have penetrated to distant villages. Mamla kat athletes got the necessary conditions to take first place in international competitions.

The adoption of the Decree of the President of the Republic of Uzbekistan on March 31, 2017 "On the establishment of the State Committee on Investments of the Republic of Uzbekistan" will fully realize the country's investment potential, further improve the investment environment, develop high-quality annual investment programs, and attract foreign investments, creating favorable conditions for international financial institutions, financial institutions of foreign governments, expanding cooperation with leading foreign companies and banking structures, as well as creating modern legal bases for increasing the effectiveness of attracted foreign investments. In the decree, the newly created State Committee on Investments was determined to be the competent state body responsible for coordinating the formation and implementation of the unified state investment policy and attracting foreign investments. The main task of this committee is to "encourage the expansion of investments in the sectors and regions of our country's economy, to further improve the investment environment in the republic, to support the development of enterprises with foreign capital, including the formation and implementation of the policy of attracting foreign investments." development and implementation of measures for further improvement of the regulatory legal framework in the field of coordinating work, attracting foreign investments and creating more favorable conditions for expanding investment activities in the territory of the Republic of Uzbekistan. In addition, according to the Decree, the decisions of the State Committee on Investments, adopted within the framework of their powers and having a normative-legal nature, are of state and economic management organizations, local state power and management organizations, regardless of the form of ownership and departmental affiliation, it must be performed by economic entities.[30]

---

adopted on February 16. February 16, 2017.//http:// www.press-service. en/ en/lists/view/257

[30] Decree of the President of the Republic of Uzbekistan on March 31, 2017 "On the establishment of the State Committee on Investments of the Republic of Uzbekistan". March 31, 2017.//http://www.press-service.uz/uz/ lists/view/366

In the Decree of the President of the Republic of Uzbekistan, adopted on April 11, 2017, "On measures to radically increase the effectiveness of the activities of internal affairs organizations, to strengthen their responsibility in ensuring public order, citizens' rights, freedoms and legal interests, in ensuring reliable protection" the following serious shortcomings and problems accumulated in the activity were shown:

- *firstly,* the main tasks and functions are not clearly divided between the republic, middle and lower level divisions, which makes it difficult to determine the priorities of each employee's activity and personal responsibility for the final result of the work;

- *secondly,* the current organizational and state structures do not ensure the rational use of forces and means, as a result of which there is not enough work volume in some services of the central and middle level, and at a time when there are more than necessary staff units, it leads to overloading of subordinate units with too many service tasks;

- *thirdly,* officials of internal affairs organizations, including preventive inspectors, have not established communication with the population, the culture of dealing with citizens remains low, effective cooperation with citizens' self-government organizations and other institutions of civil society in solving the most important problems of the population not provided;

- *fourthly,* the appeals of individuals and legal entities are considered superficially, the issues raised in them are not thoroughly analyzed in all respects. The fact that they are being answered only for the sake of insanity causes dissatisfaction of the citizens of the Republic of Uzbekistan forces to appeal to the People's Reception Offices of the President and other organizations with complaints;

- *fifthly,* an effective system of reporting of officials of internal affairs organizations to the population, effective mechanisms of public, parliamentary and parliamentary control over their activities have not been introduced, which does not allow to increase the responsibility of employees for the effective performance of the tasks assigned to them;

- *sixthly,* work on the prevention and prophylactic of crimes mainly consists of fighting against the consequences of committed illegal acts, systematic and effective on early prevention of crimes, deep analysis of the causes and conditions of their commission, identification and elimination measures are not taken;

- - *seventhly,* insufficient attention is paid to protecting the growing generation from destructive ideas, preventing youth from being involved in criminal activities, especially terrorism and religious extremism, and the educational role of internal affairs organizations is not felt;
- *eighthly,* the system of training, retraining and upgrading of the internal affairs organizations does not meet the current requirements, cases of bribery and abuse of official position still occur;
- - *ninthly,* the level of introducing the latest information and communication technologies into the system, equipping internal affairs organizations with modern tools and equipment remains unsatisfactory.

In order to eliminate the serious shortcomings and problems mentioned in the decree, and to fundamentally modernize the management of the internal affairs system, the following important directions of reform of this sector were determined:

Firstly, to transform the internal affairs organizations into a socially oriented professional structure that provides timely and quality assistance to the population, where each employee considers *serving the interests of the people* as their duty;

Secondly, taking into account the modern dangers and threats, the importance and scope of the work being performed, clearly defining and distributing the tasks and functions of internal affairs organizations at all levels, optimizing the organizational and staff structure, rational use of forces and means;

Thirdly, to ensure a systematic communication with the people aimed at a specific goal, to develop close cooperation with the self-government organizations of citizens, other institutions of civil society, to provide comprehensive assistance in solving the most important problems of the population;

Fourthly, to establish a qualitatively new procedure for organizing work with appeals from individuals and legal entities, to put an end to superficial and formalistic approaches to the review and resolution of appeals, to use all means within the scope of authority to protect the rights and legal interests of citizens;

Fifthly, to introduce a system of regular reporting of officials of internal affairs organizations to the public, clear criteria for evaluating the work done, as well as effective mechanisms of public, parliamentary and parliamentary control to ensure legality in their activities;

Sixthly, first of all, timely elimination of the causes and conditions of the commission of violations, raising the legal culture of all layers of the population, instilling in them a sense of respect for the law, intolerance to any form of violation of the law, ensuring early prevention and prevention of violations;

Seventhly, to teach minors and young people love for the Motherland, patriotism, national and universal values to educate in the spirit of respect, to develop a system aimed at protecting the growing generation from terrorism, religious extremism, violence and brutality;

Eighthly, to fundamentally revise and further improve the system of training, retraining and upgrading of the internal affairs organizations, to eliminate the reasons and conditions that lead to the commission of offenses by them;

Ninthly, widespread introduction of modern information and communication technologies, which ensure the more efficient operation of all departments of internal affairs organizations.[31]

The goals and tasks set in the decree show that in order to fundamentally change the system of the Ministry of Internal Affairs in the country, modernization of its management system and service delivery methods has begun. The management system in this field should be mainly serving the people, moving its main activities to the population, using new modern methods of ensuring the protection of citizens' rights and freedoms, giving importance to the elimination of corruption among the officials of the executive power structures, increasing the effectiveness of supervision and service delivery, and preventing crime. and the promotion of preventive work to the level of basic management activities, etc., began to bear fruit in a short period of time. Over the past year, crime has decreased by 30 percent. The system of the Ministry of Internal Affairs has begun to be renewed at the expense of quality and qualified personnel.

In the Decree of the President of the Republic of Uzbekistan on April 14, 2017 "On measures to improve the management system in the field of

---

[31] Decree of the President of the Republic of Uzbekistan "On the establishment of the State Committee on Investments of the Republic of Uzbekistan". March 31, 2017.// http://www.press-service.uz/uz/lists/view/390.

foreign trade", further increase the efficiency of foreign trade relations, liberalization of foreign trade, strengthening of export potential and in order to improve the system of releasing competitive local products to foreign markets, to form long-term stable partnership relations in the field of trade between production enterprises and foreign partners, the Ministry of Foreign Economic Relations, Investments and Trade of the Republic of Uzbekistan was reorganized into the Ministry of Foreign Trade of the Republic of Uzbekistan. Also, this ministry was provided with the status of an authorized state body, and it was determined that it is responsible for the formation and implementation of state policy in the field of foreign trade, and that it coordinates the work of state administration organizations in the field of foreign trade regulation. It was stipulated that the decisions of this Ministry, adopted within the scope of its powers and having a normative-legal nature, must be implemented by state and economic management organizations, local state power and management organizations, and economic entities, regardless of the form of ownership and departmental affiliation. The main tasks and directions of activity of this ministry were determined in particular as follows: - development and implementation of a unified state policy in the field of foreign trade activities; - to carry out comprehensive marketing research of world markets, to assist in the implementation of programs to develop the export potential of the Republic of Uzbekistan, to develop and implement practical measures to strengthen and develop the competitiveness of high-value-added products produced in the Republic of Uzbekistan, taking into account the needs of foreign markets:

- to analyze on a systematic basis the types and types of products produced by economic entities, to determine the level of their competitiveness in foreign markets, to form a relevant database;

 - supporting the export of goods, works and services, trade of the Republic of Uzbekistan with foreign countries to help expand and strengthen cooperation, to provide favorable conditions for the entry of goods, works and services produced in the Republic of Uzbekistan to foreign markets, to develop and implement activities aimed at diversification of sales markets;

- providing practical assistance to economic entities in searching for and choosing reliable foreign trade partners, as well as local enterprises' participation in tenders, international trade and industrial exhibitions, fairs and other similar events held in foreign countries;

- Developing and implementing measures for the development of the foreign trade infrastructure of the Republic of Uzbekistan, in particular, the development of transit potential, logistics and transport corridors.[32]

This Decree created the legal basis for the implementation of the management system in the field of foreign trade as a factor in the development of the market economy. If we pay more attention to the new changes in the management of the decree, it is clearly visible that the goals and tasks of the Ministry of Foreign Trade are aimed at serving entrepreneurs and farmers in the country, protecting them from external pressures and intervention of foreign goods. Adaptation of public service provision to the requirements of the market economy in the conditions of building a civil society certainly means its modernization. In this sense, the Ministry of Foreign Trade has become a structure of executive power that can create opportunities for the country to adapt to the market economy and fully join the world economic integration. "Privatized Republic of Uzbekistan" adopted by the President of the Republic of Uzbekistan on April 18, 2017

On the establishment of the state committee for assistance to enterprises and development of competition"[33], "On measures to further improve the management of the housing and communal services system" adopted on April 19,[34] and "On drinking water under the Cabinet of Ministers of the Republic of Uzbekistan" adopted on April 19 In the decrees on the establishment of the state inspection of use control,[35] focused on aspects such

---

[32] Decree of the President of the Republic of Uzbekistan "On measures to improve the management system in the field of foreign trade" adopted on April 14, 2017. April 14, 2017.// http://www.press-service.uz/uz/lists/

view/401.

[33] Decree of the President of the Republic of Uzbekistan "On the establishment of the State Committee for Assistance to Privatized Enterprises and Development of

Competition of the Republic of Uzbekistan". April 18, 2017.// http://www.press-service.uz/ en/lists/view/415.

[34] Decree of the President of the Republic of Uzbekistan "On measures to further improve the   management of housing and communal services". April 19, 2017.// http:// www.press-service.uz/uz/lists/view/417.

[35] Decree of the President of the Republic of Uzbekistan "On the establishment of the state inspection of the use of drinking water under the Cabinet of Ministers of the Republic of Uzbekistan". April 19, 2017.// http://www.

as the effective implementation of public service to citizens, focusing it on satisfying the interests and needs of the population, and quickly solving the problems that have arisen. In particular, in the Decree "On measures to further improve the management of the housing and communal services system", the following shortcomings were noted in the provision of public services by the state: "Local executive authorities, private housing owners' associations and housing does not adequately coordinate the activities of utility service organizations. The lack of a comprehensive approach to the management and use of the multi-apartment housing fund is an obstacle to the further improvement of the system of providing high-quality and guaranteed communal services to the population, and causes the rightful objections of the housing owners. Control of the maintenance of multi-apartment housing stock at an appropriate level is not organized, in many cases the technical operation of the housing stock and the safe living of the population in it, it is allowed to violate the requirements established under The rules and deadlines for the repair and restoration of buildings and structures are not being followed, the demolition of old houses is not being carried out, the condition of the areas adjacent to multi-apartment houses does not fully meet sanitary standards, rules and hygiene standards. The population is not sufficiently provided with quality drinking water and centralized heat supply.

Also, as the purpose of adopting this decree, "on the basis of close cooperation with housing and communal service organizations, to further improve the system of management and use of multi-family housing stock, to form an effective system for technical control of compliance with the rules of maintenance of multi-family houses, to inform residents to fundamentally improve the provision of high-quality housing and communal services, as well as to ensure the stable operation of housing owners' associations" and set the following goals:

- to ensure the implementation of state tenders for the construction of low-cost multi-family houses, implementation of customer functions for the construction of low-cost multi-family houses, water supply, sewage, heat supply facilities, organizing the demolition of old and dilapidated houses;

- monitoring the technical condition of multi-apartment houses, including the organization of perfect and current repair works of the multi-apartment housing fund;

press-service.uz/uz/lists/view/418.

- aligningthe activities of private housing owners' associations with the requirements for determining the costs of maintenance, use and operation of multi-apartment housing stock, rules and regulations for the technical operation of multi-apartment houses, sanitary standards, rules and regulations of areas adjacent to multi-apartment houses and control over compliance with hygiene regulations;

- schemes for the development of water supply and sewage facilities, heat supply systems in settlements, etc. developing development, modernization and reconstruction programs in connection with the plans and organizing their quality implementation, coordinating the activities of organizations in this field and ensuring management;

- implementation of resource- and energy-saving technologies and equipment to the housing and communal service system, including equipping housing and communal facilities with modern computing and measuring instruments, wide selection of local modern and high-quality building materials and products that ensure a decrease in the cost of construction and assembly works application;

- preparation of proposals for improvement of the normative legal framework in the field of housing and communal services, development and implementation of modern forms and methods of housing and communal services, taking into account the advanced experience of developed foreign countries.

All the new tasks related to the provision of communal services specified in this Decree. These are aimed at solving the most problematic situations of the present time. It defines the new directions of public utility service, improvement of houses where people live, sewerage, drinking water, and their heating. The decree focused on the modernization of public utility services by the state in the country.[36] Decree of the President of the Republic of Uzbekistan on May 2, 2017 "On measures to radically improve the activities of the State Architecture and Construction Committee of the Republic of Uzbekistan", adopted on April 21, 2017 "On the improvement of the state management system in the field of ecology and environmental protection", adopted on May 12, 2017 "On the establishment of the State Forestry Committee of the Republic of Uzbekistan", 2017. In the decrees "On measures to radically improve the

---

[36] Decree of the President of the Republic of Uzbekistan "On measures to further improve the management of the housing and communal services system". April 19, 2017

conditions for the development of information technologies in the Republic" adopted on June 30, "On efforts to further improve management in the press and information sphere", adopted on August 11, 2017, the decrees on construction, architecture, ecology, The tasks of modernization of the executive power, such as the responsibility of officials in the field of forestry, information technologies and the press, their assessment according to the results of their management activities, the non- duplication of the powers of the executive organizations, conducting the public service based on the interests of the population, and working among the population have been embodied.

According to the Decree of the President of the Republic of Uzbekistan on July 5, 2017 "On increasing the efficiency of the state policy on youth and supporting the activities of the Youth Union of Uzbekistan", the activities of the Youth Union of Uzbekistan have been terminated, and a completely new one - adapted to the relations of the market economy, and youth in the transition period The Youth Union of Uzbekistan was established to provide social protection, employ them, and help them grow their legal culture and social consciousness.

As a result of the implementation of the decree, the Youth Union of Uzbekistan became a structure that provides effective cooperation with state organizations, non-governmental non-profit organizations and other institutions of civil society in the implementation of the state policy on youth in the republic, and carries out professional activities under the slogan "Youth is the future builder" turned. In addition, the legal and practical powers of the Youth Union of Uzbekistan were expanded, and appropriate opportunities and privileges were granted in order to organize effective public control over the activities of competent agencies involved in the implementation of the state policy on youth, and to take effective measures based on the results. According to this decree, the Department of Youth Policy Issues was established in the Office of the President of the Republic of Uzbekistan. It was decided to be headed by the State Adviser of the President of the Republic of Uzbekistan on Youth Policy Issues - the Chairman of the Central Council of the Youth Union of Uzbekistan. The Youth Policy Service is responsible for the effective organization of the activities of the Central Council of the Youth Union of Uzbekistan, the organization and control of the full implementation of the tasks specified in the Law of the Republic of Uzbekistan "On State Policy Regarding Youth", the coordination of state power and management organizations, non- governmental non-profit organizations and other institutions of civil society.[37] It was decided to carry out tasks such as monitoring and coordinating their activities in this regard, organizing ideological and methodological support for them, developing proposals for improving the legal documents and law enforcement practice. In the decree, new legal statuses were formed, according to which chairmen of the councils of the Republic of Karakalpakstan, regions, the city of Tashkent, districts and cities of the Republic of Karakalpakstan, the chairman of the Council of Ministers of the Republic of Karakalpakstan, the governors of the regions, the city of Tashkent, districts and cities are considered advisers on youth policy issues, and they are equal in status to their first deputies. Also, according to the decree, the chairman of the Council of Ministers of the Republic of Karakalpakstan, the deputy of the mayors of regions, Tashkent, districts and cities for youth policy, social development and spiritual and educational affairs, the deputy of the head of district (city) internal affairs departments (departments) for youth issues. It was decided that the head of the crime prevention department (unit) will be appointed to the position based on the recommendation of the chairman of the Central Council of the Youth Union. Of course, the development of the youth self-management system and its reform in accordance with the requirements of civil society, creating opportunities for young people to express their interests in society and state administration, and giving the right to recommend candidates for positions in the field of public administration and service provision of the majority of the population. It refers to the processes of modernization of the sphere of public service provision to young people. In addition, these changes indicate that the state has switched to conducting a strong social policy towards the social stratum of the youth.

CONTROL QUESTIONS

1. What are the issues of further improvement of the neighborhood institution?
2. What does radically increase the effectiveness of internal affairs

---

[37] 2017 of the President of the Republic of Uzbekistan. Decree "On improving the efficiency of state policy on youth and supporting the activities of the Youth Union of Uzbekistan" adopted on July 5. July 5, 2017.// http:// www.press-service.uz/uz/lists/view/748.

organizations?
3. What does improving the management system in the field of foreign trade include?

9-THEME: MODERNIZATION OF THE SYSTEM OF EXECUTIVE POWER IN THE COUNTRY FORMATION OF THE NATIONAL MODEL AND ITS PROSPECTS

Plan:

1. Ideological foundations of the "Concept of Administrative Reforms in the Republic of Uzbekistan".
2. The problem of forming a new model of public administration.
3. Tasks of fundamental reform of the national system of providing public services to the population.

The legal basis and concept of modernization of the executive power system in Uzbekistan, typical of truly developed countries, began on September 8, 2017 after the adoption of the Decree of the President of the Republic of Uzbekistan "On approval of the concept of administrative reforms in the Republic of Uzbekistan". The "Concept of Administrative Reforms in the Republic of Uzbekistan", approved by this decree and developed on the basis of the ideas of President Sh.M. Mirziyoyev, emorganizations the legal basis and strategic concept of modernization of the executive power system in the country. Of course, this reality was a historical turning point in the country. Because the transformation of the executive power system into a management body working on the basis of people's interests and needs meant that the features and characteristics of a civil society and a legal state were formed in the country.

This Decree approved the "Concept of Administrative Reforms in the Republic of Uzbekistan", which aims to ensure a completely new, effective and high-quality action strategy under the supervision of the state, to organize the harmonious operation of state administration organizations and local executive authorities.

This direction of administrative reforms (the concept of "administrative" comes from the Latin "administrative" (administrate - supervision, management) concept) is also used in Western countries to modernize state power and local authorities. In this decree, the management of state authorities in the country is not at the level of the requirements of building a market economy and civil society. while noting that there are still a number of systemic problems and shortcomings that prevent the successful implementation of the state policy on modernization of economic sectors and social sphere, comprehensive development of regions, and improvement of the standard of living and well-being of the population. - opened the moon. In the decree, President Shavkat Mirziyoyev pointed out the following 11 major problems that are an obstacle to the growth of the country's economic potential and the provision of public services to citizens in this area:

Firstly, the principles of organizing the activities of the executive authorities do not ensure the timely solution of the problems accumulated in the localities, which slow down the development of the regions;

Secondly, the declarative nature of the duties assigned to some executive authorities, their implementation the lack of organizational and legal mechanisms for improvement, the duplication of tasks and the presence of cases of excess regulation by the state have a negative impact on the effectiveness of the ongoing reforms;

Thirdly, the current system of coordinating and controlling the activities of executive authorities does not ensure timely identification and elimination of systemic problems that prevent the implementation of decisions;

Fourthly, mechanisms for evaluating the performance of executive authorities consist only of recording cases and current collection of statistical data, which in most cases do not reflect the true state of affairs on the ground;

Fifthly, there is no clear boundary of the area of responsibility of the executive authorities and their leaders, especially there are no effective mechanisms of internal departmental and inter- departmental cooperation of the executive authorities;

Sixthly, excessive centralization of state functions and powers leads to a decrease in the role of local executive authorities in forming regional development programs and solving the most important problems of the population;

Seventhly, the level of introducing modern innovative methods of planning and organizing work, advanced communication technologies into the management process does not allow to ensure the effective implementation of the decisions made and to quickly monitor its process, and also causes excessive bureaucratization and high costs in public administration is happening;

Eighthly, the administration of state regulatory and economic functions by the economic management organizations, an outdated network management system that does not have sufficient flexibility and market orientation, unreasonable provision of individual preferences, preferences and advantages hinders the development of a healthy competitive environment;

Ninthly, the underdevelopment of social and public-private partnership limits the participation of non-governmental non-profit organizations and business entities in solving current socio-economic problems and, as a result, does not ensure the reduction of budget costs;

Tenthly, insufficient open and transparent functioning of executive authorities, weak mechanisms of public control lead to excessive bureaucracy and various forms of corruption;

Eleventhly, the lack of responsibility and initiative of some leaders has a negative impact on the timely and high-quality resolution of the tasks and target instructions for the complex socio-economic development of the regions.[38]

In this decree, the problems and shortcomings accumulated in the system of state and local government management at the present time, which seriously hinder administrative reforms, were revealed. In other words, in this decree, not only the tasks of implementing administrative reforms, but also the complications of the old management methods that are causing the development of these reforms, and how and in what cases they do not allow the modernization of state administration, have been thoroughly clarified. The concept of administrative reforms in the Republic of Uzbekistan can ensure the full implementation of reforms, adopted normative legal

---

[38] See: Decree of the President of the Republic of Uzbekistan "On approval of the concept of administrative reforms in the Republic of Uzbekistan" of September 8, 2017 No. PF-5185 // http://www.press-service.uz.

documents and state programs, as well as identify and effectively solve the problems of socio-political and socio-economic development in a timely manner. It was adopted in order to form a new state administration system. Its main task was to form a conceptual new model of state administration.

The concept of administrative reforms defined the strategy of reforms to be implemented in 7 directions.[39] First of all, this concept is not only the democratization of state administration, but also the architect of reforms leading to changes in all spheres of society. Modernization has set the task of building a state that exhibits the full qualities of developed states. The main goal of the concept of administrative reforms was focused on the formation of a new model of public administration in the following areas:

I. Improvement of the institutional and organizational-legal foundations of the activities of the executive authorities. This direction included the following:

• introduction of specific criteria and procedures for the establishment and termination of executive authorities, including their structural and territorial units, aimed at preventing an unjustified increase in the administrative apparatus, budget burden, and bureaucratization of state administration;

• optimization of executive authorities, their structures and departments, taking into account the elimination of imbalances between republican and regional executive authorities, as well as ensuring the proper distribution of personnel and material resources;

• revising and improving mechanisms of interaction of lower levels of executive authorities with the government, increasing their independence and responsibility;

• optimization of administrative procedures, automation of the management process;

• information exchange in order to have a timely and appropriate impact on the threats and problems arising in the regions and the whole country formation of an effective system of education, for this purpose, wider implementation of the "Electronic Government" system and modern information and communication technologies in the activities of

---

[39] Collision [lat. collisio] – 1) conflict of opposing views, aspirations and interests; 2) legal. Differences and inconsistencies of individual laws within one country, or conflicting laws and court decisions of different countries.

executive authorities at all levels;

- development of the administrative justice system by improving the procedure for appeals to higher authorities on the decisions and actions (inaction) of executive authorities and their officials, introducing mechanisms for collegial hearing of appeals of individuals and legal entities as a method of resolving disputes before the court.

II. Clarifying, aligning and improving the processes of mutual cooperation of the tasks (functions, powers) of executive authorities, their implementation mechanisms and areas of responsibility. This direction includes the following:

o defining the specific tasks (functions, powers) and area of responsibility of the executive authorities and their heads, defining the mechanisms for the implementation of each task and function, including information and analytical support, strategic planning;

o implementation of administrative procedures and regulations on project management, implementation of regulatory functions, provision of public services;

o "Department of the President of the Republic of Uzbekistan - Cabinet of Ministers - to coordinate and control the activities of executive authorities, which allows to organize the effective work of executive authorities at all levels and mobilize their forces, as well as to prevent situations of narrow departmental approach in solving tasks for the development of regions" introduction of an effective system of state administration organizations of the republic - structural and territorial divisions - local executive authorities;

o interdepartmental collegial organizations (commissions, councils, working groups, etc.) radical reduction;

o taking into account the specific characteristics of regions and the need to comprehensively solve local problems, to increase initiative and strengthen the role of regional executive authorities in the formation of state and regional development programs;

o introduction of a principled new system of evaluating the activities of executive authorities and their leaders at all levels, including program budgeting and hearing their reports by representative authorities, based on the achievement of target indicators and the effectiveness of the implementation of strategic development programs;

o It is intended to prevent the adoption of regulatory legal documents without properly assessing their impact, as well as the gradual elimination of the practice of adopting departmental regulatory legal documents that lead to conflicting norms, double interpretation, manifestations of corruption, and excessive regulation by the state. Introduction of "intelligent regulation" models and a standardized methodology of analysis of the regulatory impact of the adopted decisions, etc.

III. Further reduction of administrative influence on economic sectors and expansion of market mechanisms of management. This direction included the following:

✓ development of a healthy competitive environment in the most necessary economic sectors and social sectors (industry, transport, energy, etc.), improving the management system, focusing on eliminating the conflict of state and commercial interests;

✓ establishment of restrictions on the establishment of commercial organizations with state participation in areas where the private sector is operating effectively and reorganization of existing enterprises;

✓ control abandoning the practice of financing the authorized executive authorities at the expense of the economic management organizations under their control. Legal and institutional basis of social and public-private partnership aimed at ensuring broad participation of non-governmental organizations and business entities in solving urgent issues of socio-economic development (education, health care, tourism, communal economy, road transport infrastructure) and reducing budget costs. improvement;

✓ transferring some of them to the private sector, introducing mechanisms of state control over the proper performance of state functions through licensing, certification, accreditation and permitting procedures;

IV. Improvement of mechanisms of vertical management system and cooperation of executive authorities. This direction was mainly focused on the decentralization of the management system of state authorities. It envisages the transfer of the powers of the state administration organizations of the Republic to the local state authorities, from the region to the district (city) state authorities, the gradual decentralization of the state administration, the increase of the financial capabilities of the local state authorities, including tax allocations to the local budget, and in order to develop and implement regional development programs, by increasing the interest of local state authorities in expanding the tax base, by revising the status of the mayor as the head of the representative body of the local government, keeping the status of the head of the executive power in it, and by creating the secretariat of the Councils of People's Deputies ensuring the practical implementation of the principle of separation of powers in the organization of the state power system, regional divisions of executive power organizations of local state power organizations, especially the Ken Gash of People's Deputies to increase the role and responsibility of controlling the activities, to strengthen the powers of the local state authorities in matters of selection and placement of the management personnel of regional executive authorities by gradually transferring the relevant powers to the governor, and in the future to supervise the activities of local executive authorities and governors introducing the procedure for the election of governors aimed at ensuring effective public control, the tasks of increasing the role and efficiency of the citizens' self-government organizations in solving the current issues of social and economic development.

V. Introducing modern forms of strategic planning, innovative ideas, developments and technologies into the public administration system. This direction consisted of the following tasks:

✓ to create a strategic planning system that would allow for the formation of future models of innovative development of priority sectors and industries based on long-term scenarios of increasing the intellectual and technological potential of the country;

✓ introduction of innovative forms of state management that ensure the optimization and simplification of procedures for the provision of state services, increase the efficiency of the activities of state organizations;

✓ comprehensive support for the development of scientific research and innovative activities, including the development of innovative ideas and technologies, as well as the wide involvement of investments in it, and the formation of a regulatory legal framework that ensures their further development.

VI. Formation of an effective system of professional public service, introduction of effective mechanisms of fighting corruption in the system of executive authorities. In this direction, the following tasks were set:

✓ organization of the civil service in order to create a professional corps of civil servants, including the legal status, classification of civil servants, recruitment development of drafts of legal documents regulating the issues of transparency mechanisms (on the basis of selection), formation of personnel reserve, transfer of service, compliance with ethical norms;

✓ Establishment of a specialized body responsible for the implementation of the unified state personnel policy under the President of the Republic of Uzbekistan; development of special educational directions for training specialists in the field of public administration and improving the qualifications of civil servants, introducing modern methods of evaluating the efficiency of their activities based on personal achievements, knowledge and professional skills;

✓ creation of a modern system of remuneration and social security of civil servants, which will increase the attractiveness of public service, reduce the risk of corruption and abuse of power;

✓ to ensure the transparency and openness of the activities of executive authorities, to introduce modern forms of information provision to individuals and legal entities, to eliminate excessive administrative costs in interaction with society and business.

VII. Expected results from the implementation of administrative reforms. In this direction, the following was determined: creation of a public administration system capable of ensuring the full implementation of the expected reforms, identifying and effectively solving the problems of socio-political and socio-economic development in a timely manner, responding to the global trends of innovative development, including through:

- optimization and decentralization of the public administration system due to elimination of redundant and non-specific tasks, functions and powers, duplication and parallelism;

-making public administration free from bureaucracy and reducing its costs, increasing the efficiency and transparency of the management decision-making system;

- introduction of a system of strategic planning, innovative ideas, developments and technologies;

- to further reduce the administrative influence on economic sectors and to develop a healthy competitive environment of management, to expand the market mechanisms aimed at increasing the investment attractiveness of the country and the work activity of the population;

-introduction of effective forms of public and parliamentary control, primarily aimed at preventing corruption.

Creating effective mechanisms for ensuring the rights and freedoms of citizens, further increasing their well-being and the level of satisfaction with the activities of executive authorities, including through:

- improvement of administrative procedures aimed at clearly regulating the legal relations of state organizations with individuals and legal entities;

- development of the administrative justice system, which provides for the improvement of the procedure for appeals against the decisions and actions of the executive authorities, and the introduction of collegial hearing mechanisms for the appeals of individuals and legal entities;

- Improving the efficiency of public services by improving the "Electronic Government" system, ensuring the rule of law in society.

The essence of the concept and the tasks set in it show that it includes public administration in developed countries such as the USA, Great Britain, France, Germany, the Netherlands, Italy, Japan, and Australia, which we analyzed in chapters 1-2, living in the conditions of civil society and the rule of law. The experience of modernization combined with national traditions finds its expression in Uzbekistan. Looking at it from a wider perspective, modernization of state authorities in the country is a matter of citizenship focused on the formation of society and the legal state. Because civil society can develop not in a state with a strong executive power, but in the conditions of a modernized legal state. It is known that the formation of the civil society creates the conditions for the activities of the people to be based on national interests, social stability and people's well-being, which are important for human development. Because, in the conditions of the civil society, where the interests of the society and the interests of the individual are combined, the tendency of citizens to join human units based on the rights and interests and to control the authorities and participate in them was formed and grew.

Based on the "Concept of Administrative Reforms in the Republic of Uzbekistan", on December 12, 2017, the Decree of the President of the Republic of Uzbekistan "On measures to radically reform the national system of public services to the population" was adopted. It is known that within a short period of one year, comprehensive measures aimed at improving the quality of service activities of state organizations, creating optimal conditions and facilities for providing state services to business entities on the "one-stop" principle have been implemented. In particular, from February 1, 2017, the transfer of the single centers for providing public services to business entities from the structure of district and city governments to the Ministry of Justice of the Republic of Uzbekistan under the principle of "one-stop shop" is an important step in the development of this sector, the formation of another vertical structure, their effective made it possible to organize its activities. As a result, the number of public services provided by these centers has increased to 33. Starting from April 1, 2017, the automated system of state registration of business entities, which allows to reduce the registration procedure to 30 minutes, was launched. Doing Business 2018 global rating served to improve the position of Uzbekistan from 24th to 11th place according to the "Business Registration" indicator. At the same time, the results of open dialogue with the people and the analysis of the practice of protecting citizens' rights showed that there are some systemic problems in the transition of the national system of public services to a new level in terms of quality that fully satisfies the needs of the population and business entities. First of all, conditions were created for the use of the state service provision system by the "single window" principle. Citizens were faced with various bureaucratic obstacles due to the complex procedures for issuing documents in various state organizations and organizations. Also, the lack of information systems, resources and databases in public service organizations, as well as the low level of their inter-departmental integration, complicated the situation and did not allow for convenient and timely use of all public services.

In addition, the procedures for the provision of most public services remain complex and difficult for citizens to use, and their pricing mechanisms are not transparent. As a result, narrow departmental interests did not give the opportunity to fully satisfy the interests of citizens. Citizens are often faced with financial costs when applying to state organizations, and as a result of the low level of introduction of information and communication technologies in this area, long-term circulation of paper documents, a long time was spent waiting in line for decisions. Failure to create an effective system of control and quality assessment of public services through remote monitoring and public opinion polling had a negative impact on the effectiveness of ensuring legitimacy in the field of public services.

The Decree of the President of the Republic of Uzbekistan "On Measures to Fundamentally Reform the National System of Providing Public Services to the Population" adopted on February 12, 2017 is a complex external legal measure to fundamentally increase the quality, speed, transparency and accessibility of public services.

- he created the mechanism for the implementation of events, the main ideas that implicitly implement the grand idea that "government agencies should serve our people, not the people". In order to modernize the system of providing public services to the population, a separate state body was established

- mainly the State Services Agency under the Ministry of Justice of the Republic of Uzbekistan and its regional units.[40]

According to the decree, it was established that the "single window" principle applies not only to business entities, but also directly to citizens. Citizens now have the opportunity to apply to executive state structures without communicating directly with state officials, a mechanism has been created to ensure citizens' communication with state organizations, the opportunity to provide fast and corruption-free services to the population has arisen, conditions that ease the daily life of citizens, free from bureaucracy and bureaucracy. Conditions have been created. The past short period has shown that the active participation of a special institution in the provision of public services - Public receptions of the President of the Republic of Uzbekistan is one of the most important innovations. In the decree, the factors of increasing the effectiveness of public service provision were determined for the unified operation of public reception centers and state service centers at the district and city levels. As an effective mechanism of electronic cooperation of citizens with state organizations, the creation of a single register of State services, development of single administrative regulations for each type of state services, information systems, resources, databases and software products in the Agency, its regional offices and state service centers, as well as the implementation of measures for the introduction of hardware and software complexes was determined. The important principle that "documents move, not citizens" was introduced in the provision of public services. Citizens can use internet and mobile technology services, state services can be provided remotely by electronic communication.

The decree provides for the creation of mechanisms for speedy implementation and quality improvement of public services in the field of public services, including healthcare, licensing, taxation, customs and other areas, as well as the development of mobile applications for public services, providing services to remote areas. , to create an opportunity to establish fast relations with the population, to organize an effective system of bilateral relations with the help of official websites and social networks.

---

[40] Decree of the President of the Republic of Uzbekistan "On measures to radically reform the national system of blind sale of public services to the population". December 12, 2017.//https://kun.uz/news/2017/ 12/13/ the president's new decree was approved.

In addition, the list of 58 new public services, which will be provided at the State Service Centers on the basis of the "single window" principle, was approved in 2018-2020. Among them are water supply to houses, connection to sewerage, heat supply and other engineering and communication networks, obtaining a permit for individual housing construction, registration (propiska), deregistration and registration, various archives. The application of the type of public services, such as obtaining duplicates of references, patents, certificates and official documents, was established.[41]

The Decree of the President of the Republic of Uzbekistan on April 11, 2018 "On additional measures to accelerate the development of the state service delivery system" initiated a new stage of modernization of the executive power and its local structures. The decree noted that there are still untapped opportunities and unsolved problems in the field of public services as follows:

First of all, issues of introducing basic information systems in a number of organizations and their low level of interdepartmental integration do not ensure convenient and timely provision of public services. The indicated shortcomings are especially relevant to the Ministry of Defense, Ministry of Housing and Communal Services, Ministry of Higher and Secondary Special Education, Ministry of Construction, JSC "Uztransgaz" and local state authorities at all levels;

Secondly, the fact that the registers of information about natural and legal persons, real estate objects and other documents are kept by state organizations in separate paper form, and the absence of electronic archives lead to difficulties in providing electronic state services. This kind of negative practice is especially related to the State Committee for Land Resources, Geodesy, Cartography and State Cadastre (hereinafter referred to as the "Davergeodezka Dastr") and the "Ozarkhiv" agency;

Thirdly, most public service centers are still not connected to a high-speed Internet network, which is the reason why inter- agency electronic cooperation cannot be established at the required level. The heads of the Agency, the Ministry of Information Technologies and Communications Development, and JSC "Uzbektelecom" are not taking effective measures to eliminate these serious problems;

---

[41] Decree of the President of the Republic of Uzbekistan "On measures to radically reform the national system of blind sale of public services to the population". December 12, 2017.//https://kun.uz/news/2017/ 12/13/ the president's decree was approved

Fourthly, the competent organizations providing public service and public service centers are not adequately equipped with modern computer equipment and technical tools are the obstacle to the introduction of advanced and innovative methods of providing public services;

Fifthly, the lack of provision of the necessary buildings and rooms by the public service centers does not allow to provide full and simultaneous coverage of visitors to provide many services in high demand;

Sixthly, the passage of authorization and licensing processes remains complicated and over-regulated, the presence of excessive requirements and barriers in the process of obtaining public services leads to the loss of transparency, the practice of different application of the law and, as a result, the frequent occurrence of abuses and other violations;

Seventhly, the level of knowledge and skills of individuals and legal entities in the use of information technologies remains low, there is no organized system for teaching them to submit and receive documents in electronic form.[42]

In order to ensure rapid transition of the national system of providing public services to the population to a qualitatively new stage, as well as to consistently implement the Strategy of Actions and the Concept of Administrative Reforms in the five priority areas of development of the Republic of Uzbekistan in 2017-2021, the decree determined the following:

The following should be considered the first-level tasks of the State Services Agency, Davergeodezkadastr, "Ozarkhiv" Agency, as well as ministries and agencies in the field of public services, and other authorized organizations providing public services under the Ministry of Justice:

- rapid development and introduction of information and communication technologies, taking into account the provision of a unified technological approach to the creation of information systems and information resources in order to further unify and automate the processes of

---

[42] Decree of the President of the Republic of Uzbekistan on April 11, 2018 "On additional measures for the rapid development of the state service delivery system". April 11, 2018. //National database of legal documents (www.lex.uz)// People's word, April 12, 2018.

providing public services;
- to accelerate the implementation of measures to transfer the archive fund of ministries and agencies to a digital format and to provide access to relevant information resources;
- by reengineering business processes for all public services included in the unified state register, radically reduce procedures and deadlines for providing public services, significantly optimize forms and forms;

- to ensure that the employees involved in the process of providing public services fulfill their duties unconditionally, on time and with quality, to strengthen their responsibility, to improve their work skills and culture in accordance with the requirements of the present time, to introduce mechanisms for objective assessment of their work;
- to increase the responsibilities of state organizations and organizations in connection with the participation in the provision of public services in solving problems based on assigned tasks and functions.

To ensure further acceleration of the introduction of public services in the future and to identify weaknesses in their provision, the following procedure should be established:

- from June 1, 2018, 70-100 types of high-demand public services will be provided by state service centers according to the list in the appendix;
- on state services introduced as an experiment Protection of the rights of citizens, individuals and legal entities of the Office of the President of the Republic of Uzbekistan temporary administrative regulations approved by the head of the service for control and compliance with applications are adopted;
- the list of state services to be introduced as an experiment is formed based on the actual needs of the population and is approved by the service of the Office of the President of the Republic of Uzbekistan for the protection of citizens' rights, control and coordination of work with the appeals of individuals and legal entities based on the proposal of the Ministry of Justice of the Republic of Uzbekistan;
- public services included in the list of public services to be introduced as an experiment are provided only through public service centers;
- it is forbidden to accept applications for the provision of public services directly from the applicants by the authorized body from the day of the introduction of the provision of public services as an experiment.

State organizations and other organizations providing state services should provide:

- step by step digitization of the information stored in paper form, necessary for the provision of public services, with the aim of forming electronic databases and establishing interdepartmental electronic cooperation;

- optimization of the provided public services with the aim of eliminating redundant procedures and reducing bureaucratic elements, and according to the results, in agreement with the Ministry of Information Technologies and Communications Development of the Republic of Uzbekistan and the Ministry of Justice, developing action plans for their electronic conversion;

- integration of their departmental information systems and resources with "Electronic Government" and Agency information systems.

To approve the proposal of the Ministry of Justice of the Republic of Uzbekistan to establish the Information and Analysis Multimedia Center (hereinafter referred to as the Multimedia Center) in the form of a state institution consisting of 5 staff members, equipped with the latest information technologies and digital equipment.

The following are the main tasks of the multimedia center:

- implementation of systematic measures to increase legal awareness and legal culture among the population, especially young people, as well as in rural areas;

- conveying to the public and business entities the essence of innovations on the simplification of administrative procedures in the field of public service provision using modern technologies and creative approaches;

- preparation and transmission of information-analytical and visual media materials, including audio and video clips, TV and radio shows, social advertisements, reports from the scene of the incident, as well as to the Internet, on the broad coverage of the activities of judicial organizations and institutions;

- providing advice to the public on the procedure for using public services, including a clear and detailed explanation of the requirements of the adopted administrative regulations;

- studies and inspections of the activities of state organizations and other organizations in the provision of public services by the competent authorities in order to prevent violations, as well as informing the population about gross violations and systemic deficiencies, measures taken against the guilty, and the restored rights of the applicants;

- establishing communication with all strata of the population, studying the need for public services, social networks and to discuss among the public the most serious shortcomings of this industry through the wide use of mobile applications.[43]

The substance of the Presidential Decree shows that a system of executive power is being formed in Uzbekistan, which is typical of a legal state and civil society. First of all, this is reflected in the reforms to adapt the main activities of the executive power and its local structures to the provision of public services to the population; secondly, in the process of modernization in this field, in addition to national traditions, the experiences of modernization of the executive power system of Western countries, the USA, Japan, and South Korea are being used effectively; thirdly, for the first time in the history of our country, public administration and service activities are focused on serving the people; fourthly, as a result of citizens' appeals to the Presidential and People's Reception Offices, State Service Agencies, which deliver information on the activities of state authorities and abuse of their official duties, not only public control over the activities of the executive power, maybe citizen control is being implemented; As a result of the implementation and implementation of a series of decrees adopted by the President, the use of the powers of the officials of the executive power system based only on the interests of citizens was formed as a unique national experience, a legal and social system that does not create social evils such as the abuse of powers by officials, giving in to corruption, and putting their own interests first. norms and documents began to show their effect, aspects of public service provision specific to civil society were formed.

In the context of civil society, as we have seen above, the powers of the central government are transferred to local authorities and institutions of civil society. This situation made it necessary for the fu karos themselves to personally participate in the governing organizations. Such partnership of citizens with the state ensures stability of mutual consensus.

An important aspect of administrative reforms is that the principle of self-management of society is strengthened due to the fact that it greatly limits the activity of public authorities. The most important thing is that citizens who have achieved self-actualization in life develop the qualities of freedom and personal initiative. This situation has a direct impact on increasing the

---

[43] Decree of the President of the Republic of Uzbekistan on April 11, 2018 "On additional measures for the rapid development of the state service delivery system". April 11, 2018. //National database of legal documents (www.lex.uz)// People's word, April 12, 2018.

economic potential of the society. In addition, the feeling of free expression of desires and interests in a person increases his desire for well-being.

CONTROL QUESTIONS

1. What are the ideological foundations of the "Concept of Administrative Reforms in the Republic of Uzbekistan"?
2. What are the problems of forming a new model of public administration?
3. What are the tasks of fundamental reform of the national system of providing public services to the population?

CONCLUSION

In Great Britain, the "Citizens' Charter" program, adopted by the government in 1991, fundamentally changed the relationship between public agencies and the population. The main principles of the Charter were as follows: setting standards - setting, monitoring and announcing certain service standards expected by users of public services; Shaff ofl ik - delivering complete and accurate information to the population quickly and without any obstacles. In this case, communal and social service works, their prices, managers of these services should be conveniently delivered to everyone, etc. Since 2010, the government has cut spending, raised taxes, and implemented the largest post-World War II reforms in social security, health care, public education, and the police service. In essence, these reforms were evaluated as a reconstruction of the welfare state.

Modernization of state authorities in the USA began in 1993. The government has tasked all federal agencies with adapting to the needs of citizens and thinking less about their own interests. Most government officials have greatly increased the types of services provided to citizens, and for this purpose have switched to cooperation with private companies. The main idea of the reform strategy was aimed at strengthening relations between the government and the people, making political programs universal and understandable.

In the USA, significant attention was paid to improving the qualifications of the highest levels of state leadership. The following new directions of reforms have been defined:

- transforming the agencies most demanded by citizens into fast and efficient administrative structures that can quickly adapt to the needs of the population;
- development of "preventive" management aimed at eliminating administrative problems;
- to give civil servants the right to act more freely in connection with the increased responsibility for the results of their work;
- development of information provision and service provision.

In the USA, new important principles of state administration were formed:

- formation of effective structures instead of formal state management structures;
- strengthen competition, not monopoly;
- focus on customer needs rather than bureaucratic structures;
- to pay attention to the income of the citizens, not the scale of consumption;
- decentralization of state authorities.

In France, in 1983, a special law was adopted on the harmonization of relations between state organizations and self-government organizations, and the powers of self-government organizations were expanded: they were given the right to dispose of material resources and financial resources. This law stated the principle that the rights of self-governance given to communes, departments and regions cannot be taken over by any of them.

Administrative reforms in France began to focus mainly on the development of management and the creation of the French model of the information state. The government's strategy in this area focused on increasing the types of public services for the population, bringing the government closer to the population, and seriously democratizing the administration. Administrative reforms in France brought management and state organizations closer to each other in the business sector and served the population. It improved the quality of presentation and accelerated the execution of contractual obligations.

During this period, several measures were taken to improve the quality of services provided by the public service to the population. In particular, publishing information for citizens, holding open-door days, distributing advertising materials in areas where public service is performed, and encouraging public service employees based on letters of thanks from citizens on Internet sites. Another innovation in this area is bringing public service closer to customers. The priorities of the reforms of the modernization of public authorities in France were to make the activities of civil servants more effective and qualitative, to strengthen the democratic foundations of public administration, and to make the public service work close to the population and with effective results.

In Germany, the modernization of state authorities began in the 90s of the 20th century. During this period, the ideas of new social management (SME) began to spread widely in Europe. In the reforms, the responsibility of local communities (the lowest self-governing organizations) was given the following powers:

- private - the community can choose personnel on its own initiative, motivate them and dismiss them;
- financial - the right to dispose of revenues and expenses collected;
- organizational - authority to adapt its internal structure based on local conditions;
- making decisions in the legal and communal sphere, implementing useful constructions in one's territory;
- tax - raising or lowering community fees, collecting various contributions, collecting internal taxes and other revenues from citizens in their territory.

In Germany, administrative reforms focused on the implementation of less bureaucratic and less expensive forms of governance in cities and communities. Guaranteed services are provided instead of expensive services efforts were made to create competitiveness between them.

The new management model in Germany differs from the more rigid Anglo-Saxon model, which is based on the gradual assimilation of business management into municipal administration. Privatization has also become an important direction of work in the utility sector in Germany. The results of this modernization were also important in increasing Germany's economic power. A distinctive feature of the administrative reforms in China is that it is aimed at implementation within the framework of the Chinese Communist Party (CCP), which decided to build a "socialist market economy". In the modernization of the Chinese state executive power, as a market tool, it is planned to widely use macroeconomic adjustment of the state for the optimal distribution of resources in the country. The goal of the administrative reforms was to increase the efficiency of management with the help of macro-adjustment and indirect control from direct administrative control.

The main directions of modernization of public administration and service in China were as follows: reducing the number of the state apparatus; reorganization of the state council; developing a new effective HR policy through careful selection, training, training and placement of personnel.

In short, over the past 40 years in China, modernization of state administration and service, adaptation of the socialist structure (state organizations) to the capitalist basis (market economic relations), development of the market economy in all aspects of society, giving up the function of state organizations to lead the society and aligning it the strengthening of the funk lines began to pay off. Management functions are the lowest management organizations, enterprises, firms and as a result of giving it to companies, it strengthened the personal initiative of civil servants and employed people.

Evaluation of the administration based on the last results increased its responsibility to the population. In general, the unique Chinese model of modernization of public administration and service cannot be found in other countries of the world.

The Japanese state was the first among the Eastern countries to carry out modernization reforms of public authorities starting from the 80s of the 20th century. Japan has benefited from the experience of Western countries. Since 1990, the Japanese government has begun to introduce a national spirit into the process of modernization of public authorities. This was mainly seen in the creation of "lifetime employment" contracts between employees and managers, the creation of various benefits for senior citizens in enterprises and organizations, the principle of slow advancement of the career of an employee or servant, and the turning of national values into guiding principles, such as paying serious attention to corporate organization.

Also, in Japan, national ideas were deeply absorbed into the system of state authorities and business management. The formation of national Japanese technology based on the combination of Japanese spirit and foreign technology was one of the most important directions of the national idea. In particular, the place of work, its name, and pride in its products have been raised to the level of national values. Getting the status of "Japanese brand" in all fields has become a strategy of national management. As a result, Japan became one of the most developed countries in 20 years.

LIST OF USED LITERATURE

1. Constitution of the Republic of Uzbekistan. - Tashkent: Uzbe Kiston, 2017.

2. Decision of the President of the Republic of Uzbekistan on June 23, 2008 "On the establishment of a research center on the democratization and liberalization of judicial legislation and ensuring the independence of the judicial system" // www.lex.uz.

3. The constitutional law of the Republic of Uzbekistan "On renewal and further democratization of state administration and strengthening the role of political parties in the modernization of the country" // Collection of legal documents of the Republic of Uzbekistan. – 2007, No. 15, Article 151.

4. The constitutional law of the Republic of Uzbekistan "On the results of the referendum and the main principles of the organization of state power" // Bulletin of the Oliy Majlis of the Republic of Uzbekistan, 2002, No. 4-5, Article 60.

5. The Law of the Republic of Uzbekistan "On Openness of Activities of State Power and Management Organizations" adopted on March 11, 2014 // http:// senat.gov.uz.

6. The Law of the Republic of Uzbekistan "On Electronic Government" adopted on December 9, 2015 // http:// parlament.gov.uz.

7. Decree of the President of the Republic of Uzbekistan "On the Strategy of Actions for Further Development of the Republic of Uzbekistan" adopted on February 7, 2017 // Collection of legal documents of the Republic of Uzbekistan, 2017, No. 6, Article 70.

8. The Law of the Republic of Uzbekistan "On Combating Corruption" adopted on January 3, 2017 // Collection of Laws of the Republic of Uzbekistan, 2017, No. 1.

9. Decree of the President of the Republic of Uzbekistan dated February 3, 2017 "On measures to further improve the neighborhood institution" // Collection of Laws of the Republic of Uzbekistan, 2017, No. 6.

10. Decree of the President of the Republic of Uzbekistan "On approval

of the concept of administrative reforms of the Republic of Uzbekistan" adopted on September 8, 2017 // http://www.press-ser vice.uz.

11. Law of the Republic of Uzbekistan "On self-management organizations of citizens" (new version) // Website of the National Database of Legal Documents of the Republic of Uzbekistan - www.lex.uz.

12. Decree of the President of the Republic of Uzbekistan on December 12, 2017 "On measures to fundamentally reform the national system of providing public services to the population" // https://kun.uz.

13. Karimov IA of the Senate of the Oliy Majlis of the Republic of Uzbekistan speech at the first meeting. January 22, 2015 // http://www.uza.uz.

14. Karimov IA Our main goal is democratization and renewal of society, modernization and reform of the country: report at the joint session of the Legislative Chamber and Senate of the Oliy Majlis of the Republic of Uzbekistan. January 28, 2005 // www.press-service.uz.

15. Karimov IA Concept of further deepening of democratic reforms and development of civil society in our country: report at the joint meeting of the Legislative Chamber and the Senate of the Republic of Uzbekistan. November 12, 2010 // www.press-service.uz.

16. Karimov IA Modernization of our country and establishment of a strong civil society is our priority: report at the joint meeting of the Legislative Chamber and the Senate of the Oliy Majlis of the Republic of Uzbekistan. January 27, 2010 // www.press-service.uz.

17. Mirziyoyev Sh.M. At the solemn ceremony dedicated to the 24th anniversary of the adoption of the Constitution of the Republic of Uzbekistan lecture. December 7, 2016. // Resolutely continuing our path of national development, we will raise it to a new level. Volume 1.-T: Uzbekistan, 2017. - P.100-130.

18. Mirziyoyev Sh.M. Together we will build a free and prosperous democratic society. Report at the joint session of the chambers of the Oliy Majlis dedicated to the ceremonial inauguration of the President of the Republic of Uzbekistan. December 14, 2016 // We will resolutely continue our path of national development and raise it to a new level. Volume 1. - T: Uzbekistan, 2017. - P.131-165.

19. Mirziyoyev Sh.M. Deepening democratic reforms, ensuring

sustainable development is a guarantee of creating a decent standard of living for our people. Movement of entrepreneurs and businessmen - speech at the 8th Congress of the Liberal-Democratic Party of Uzbekistan. October 19, 2016. // We will resolutely continue our path of national development and raise it to a new level. Volume 1. - T: Uzbekistan, 2017. - P.41-94.

20. Mirziyoyev Sh.M. Ensuring the rule of law and human interests is the guarantee of the country's development and people's wellbeing. - T: Oz Bekiston, 2017. - 48 p.

21. Mirziyoyev Sh.M. Critical analysis, strict discipline and personal responsibility should be the daily rule of every leader's activity.-T: Uzbekistan, 2017. - p. 104.

22. Mirziyoyev Sh.M. Our great future is brave and noble we will build together with our people. - T: Uzbekistan, 2017. - p. 488.

23. Mirziyoyev Sh.M. His speech at the solemn ceremony dedicated to the 25th anniversary of the adoption of the Constitution of the Republic of Uzbekistan. December 7, 2017. // http://www.press-service.uz.

24. Resolutely continuing our path of national development we will raise to the stage. Volume 1. - T: Uzbekistan, 2017. - P.100-130.

25. Abu Nasr Farabi. City of virtuous people. - Tashkent: A. Qadiri People's Heritage Publishing House, 1993. p.186.

26. Aristotle. Politika // Sochineniya: V 4 t. T. 4. - Moscow: Misl, 1983. - P.513-514.

27. Analyticheskaya zapiska po itogam raboti project "Institutsio nalniy, pravovoy i ekonomicheskiy federalizm v Rossiyskoi Federatsii". - Moscow, 2006.

28. Weber M. Izbrannye proizvedeniya: Per. s german./Sost., obsh.ed. i poslesl. Yu. N. Davidova; Predisl. PP Gaydenko. - Moscow: Progress, 1990.

29. Vasiliev SV, Zhukovsky AI, Surker K. Eff ektivnost raboti organizatsiy gosudarstvennogo i munitsipalnogo upravleniya i ix slu jashikh. Veliky Novgorod: 2002. – 70 p.

30. Vasilenko IA Administrativno-gosudarstvennoye upravleniye v stranax Zapada: SSHA, Great Britain, France, Germany. – Moscow: Logos, 2010. – P. 68–74.

31. Hobbs T. Leviathan, ili Materia, forma i vlast gosudarstva serkovnogo i grajdanskogo // Hobbs T. Sochineniya: V 2 t. - T. 2. - Moscow: Misl, 1991. - 522 p.

32. Garbuzov VN Sotsialno-ekonomicheskaya model SSHA // Obshestvo i ekonomika, 2014. – C. 228–277.

33. Dadasheva A. Emergence and development of representative organizations of local state power in the Republic of Uzbekistan. - Tashkent: National University of Uzbekistan named after Mirzo Ulugbek, 2009. p. 148.

34. Yeremyan VV Local self-government and municipal management in Latin America. Istoricheskiy opit genesis: Monograph fi ya. - Moscow, 1999.

35. Ismailova G. State legal directions of liberalization of activities of local state power and self-government organizations in Uzbekistan. - Tashkent: Academy of Public Administration under the President of the Republic of Uzbekistan, 2014. p. 167.

36. Information on basic research of expert-analytical enterprise «Obespecheniye realizatsii Federalnogo zakona ot 6-ok Tyabrya 2003 g. No. 131-ӱӱ "Ob obshikh prinsikh organizatsii mestnogo self-government in the Russian Federation" in 2007.

37. Information on the implementation of the Federal Law of October 6, 2003 No. 131-FZ "Ob obshikh prinsipakh organizatsii mestnogo self-government in the Russian Federation" in 2007. Ministry of Regional Development of the Russian Federation, 2008.

38. Issledovaniye OON na temu elektronnogo pravitelstva – https :// public administration.un.org /Reports/UN-E-Government-Survey-2014 (data obrascheniya: 23.04.2016).

39. *Karchevskaya SA, Khvorostukhina DS* Finansovoye obes cheniye reform of local self-government. Finance. No. 4, 2008.

40. *Krasilnikov DG, Sivinseva OV, Troiskaya Ye. A.* Sovremen nie zapadnie upravlencheskiye model: synthesis of New Public Management and Good Governance – Ars Administrandi, 2014, #2. – P.45–62.

41. *Locke Dj.* Dva tractata o pravlenii // Sochineniya: V 4 t. - M.: Mysl, 1988. - T. 3. - P. 347,348, 349.

42. *Lexin VN, Shvetsov AN* Gosudarstvo i regiony: teoriya i

praktik gosudarstvennogo regulirovaniya territorialnogo razvitiya. - Moscow: USSR, 1997.

43.   *Lapteva L. Ye.* Rossiyskoye self-management v kontekte miro vogo opita // Mestnoye self-management: sovremenniy rossiyskiy opit zakonodatelnogo regulirovaniya. - Moscow, 998.

44.   *Lebedeva ML* French municipal system - practical application in modern Russia. Moscow: FGOU VPO "Moskovskiy gosudarstvenniy universitet prirodoobustroystva", 2007.

45.   *Mamatov H.* Legal culture, its society and the state position in the uterus. - T., 2008. - 144 p.

46.   *Mamatov H.* Legal culture and citizenship in Uzbekistan problems of the formation of society. - Tashkent, 2009. p. 256.

47.   *Montesquieu Sh.L.* Izbrannie proizvedeniya // Obsh. ed. i input St. MP Baskina. - Moscow: Goslitizdat, 1955.

48.   *Matveyev MN* Yavlyayetsya li mestnoye self-government v Rossii chastyu mestnogo gosudarstvennogo upravleniya? // Vestnik SamGU. – 2005. – No. 4 (38).

49.   *Manning N., Parison N.* Reformi gosudarstvennogo uprav leniya: mejdunarodnyy opit. - Moscow, 2003. - P.17-45.

50.   *Okuneva TV* Concept of civil society: sociological analysis // Sotsiologicheskiy almanakh. – 2013. – No. 4. p. 128.

51.   Rukovodstvo po upravleniyu obshestvennimi fi nansami at regional and municipal levels. Upravleniye budgetnimi doho dami i zaimstvovaniyami / Pod obshey redaksiyey AM Lavrova. - Moscow, 2008

52.   Roziyev Z. Citizens themselves in the protection of human rights role of self-management organizations. - Tashkent, 2012. p. 192.

53.   Rousseau JJ Obshestvennom dogovore. Treatise / Per. s fr. - Moscow, 1998. p. 54.

54.   The problem of the reform of local self-government: strukturnie i fi nansovie aspect / I. Starodubrovskaya, M. Slavgorodskaya, T. Le tunova, N. Mironova, E. Slek, G. Kitchen, J. Gabouri, F. Vaillancourt. - Moscow, 2005.

55. Sistema municipalnogo upravleniya: Uchebnik dlya vuzov / Edited by VB Zotova. - SPb., 2005. - 17 p.
56. Salikov DX Administrativnie reformi v Velikobritanii na rubeje vekov // Vestnik Chelyabinskogo gosudarstvennogo universiteta. – 2014. – No. 2. – P. 121–124.
57. Torakulov M. Civil society and local government in Uzbekistan. - Tashkent, 2009. p. 124.
58. Khristenko V. Mejbudjetnie atnoshenia i upravleniye regio nalnimi fi nansami: opit, problem, perspective. - Moscow, 2002.
59. Khakimov R. Parliament in the system of state power: problems of theory and practice. - Tashkent, 2012. p. 184.
60. Khakimov RR Improvement of legal mechanisms of ensuring cooperation between branches of state power: Monograph. - Tashkent: Sparks of Literature, 2016. p. 216.
61. Khlisheva Ye.V. Dinamika multikulturnix modeley v stranax Azii // Caspian region: politics, economy, culture. – 2012. – No. 1. – P.233–241.
62. Ugly V.Ye. Gosudarstvennoye i municipalnoye upravleniye: Uchebnik. - Moscow: Jurist, 2003. - 6 p.
63. Shtompka P. Modernization kak sotsialnoye stanovleniye (10 theses po modernizatsii) // Economic and social change: facts, trends, forecast. – 2013. – No. 6(30). – P.119–126.
64. Kyrgyzboyev M. Civil society: genesis, formation and development. - Tashkent: Uzbekistan, 2010. p. 256.
65. Finansovie aspekti vzaimodeystviya organov vlasti i mestnogo self- government / Pod redaksiyey VV Klimanova. - Moscow: USSR, 2005.]

Electronic resources

1. www.albany.edu/womeningov;
2. www.americanvalues.org;
3. www.civilfund.ru;
4. www.icscentre.org;
5. www.igh.ru;
6. www.igpran.ru;
7. www.ilscnicaragua.org;
8. www.iphras.ru;
9. www.law.umn.edu;
10. www.cei.org;
11. www.socialresearch.no;
12. www.dba.uz;
13. www.gov.uz;
14. www.infoxs.uz;
15. www.ziyonet.uz

www.ingramcontent.com/pod-product-compliance
Lightning Source LLC
LaVergne TN
LVHW010223070526
838199LV00062B/4700